How to Have A Good Year Every Year

THE FOUR-POINT POWER PLAN FOR MAXIMUM PERFORMANCE

DAVE YOHO AND JEFFREY P. DAVIDSON

BERKLEY BOOKS, NEW YORK

HOW TO HAVE A GOOD YEAR EVERY YEAR

A Berkley Book / published by arrangement with
the authors

PRINTING HISTORY
Berkley edition / March 1991

ISBN: 0-425-12685-4

A BERKLEY BOOK ® TM 757,375
Berkley Books are published by The Berkley Publishing Group,
200 Madison Avenue, New York, New York 10016.
The name "BERKLEY" and the "B" logo
are trademarks belonging to Berkley Publishing Corporation.

PRINTED IN THE UNITED STATES OF AMERICA

10 9 8 7 6 5 4

ACKNOWLEDGMENTS

This book was made possible by a great team.

My parents, my sisters, and my grandparents gave me my history.

My mentors, Aaron Jacoby, Bill McGrane, and my wife, Carole, laid the groundwork.

My many clients and business associates provided the data input.

My children, David, Adele, Tracey, and Brad, as always, were my encouragement.

Jeff Davidson, my coauthor, had the patience and foresight to work with me.

Lillian Ruzicka, Gabriela Bishop, and Carole Ann Maier, my secretaries, suffered through the dictation, the editing and re-editing.

And, of course—you, the reader, had the motivation to acquire the book and use it for the purpose for which it was written.

To Carole, without whom
life and loving could not
have been as they are

Contents

Introduction
Why the EPOD Theory?

Do not inflate plain things
into marbles, but reduce
marbles to plain things.
            —Francis Bacon

Today, many executives, entrepreneurs, and career professionals face an array of business and career-related problems. Some problems seem to have no solution or are not easily answered: How can I be an effective leader to a distracted staff? How can I get a productive eight hours from my employees? How can I be competitive and stay profitable? How can I develop and follow an effective long-range plan?

One's personal challenges can be no less taxing: How can I maintain an optimistic, positive outlook about my career? What can I do to improve my interpersonal skills? How can I initiate workable agreements and contracts? What can I do to accelerate my progress toward goals?

In the midst of an uneven economy and intensifying domestic and worldwide competition, success is an illusive concept. For a business, success means profits. For an individual, success means career advancement and fulfillment. As a consultant to hundreds of businesses, I have found that no matter what kind of success you're seeking, it will be most profoundly affected by the deployment of human resources—either your own or your business's.

Think of all the aspects of business life that involve human resources: interaction between individuals and departments; communication between personnel, customers, and vendors; and business policies—how staff, customers and community are regarded. It's the human side of business that can make or break a company or career.

Who controls the human side of business? You do. And this book will give you four essential tools that will help you create and use the human resources around you. They are: energy, persuasion, optimism, and discipline. The proper application of these elements serves as the common denominator for all thriving businesses and successful individuals.

THE EPOD THEORY

This book will enable you to gain an in-depth understanding of how energy, persuasion, optimism, and discipline affect your business or career. You'll learn how these elements can be properly applied in crucial areas and how they will become your keys to thriving *regardless* of the state of the economy or your level of competition.

For years, I wondered why some businesses and individuals thrived despite obvious limitations, while others blessed with considerable resources did not approach the success one might expect. I also wanted to identify what had led me to prosperity, and what had brought me hardship, pain, and despair, so I could share the lessons with others.

After much examination and research, I was able to view success as the proper application of four basic elements, which I call the EPOD Theory. The EPOD Theory in operating a business, managing a staff, or advancing your career represents the synthesis of my studies in business and psychology, and my thirty-two years as a business owner, consultant and speaker to both large and small organizations throughout North America, Europe and Australia.

When I bought into my first company, in 1958, the

annual sales volume was $350,000. For 22 years we averaged 26% annual growth (including acquisitions). When I began selling my interests in 1980, combined annual sales volume was $60,000,000. Since 1980, I've been a full-time speaker and trainer, while maintaining a successful consulting firm, helping thousands of executives, salespeople, and aspiring individuals.

THE FOUR ELEMENTS

Here is a brief introduction to the four EPOD Theory elements:

Energy. The energy of an individual or business can be measured by the degree of intensity, enthusiasm, and excitation that is displayed in the interaction between the individual or business and others in the transmission of ideas, the buying and selling of products or services, and the receiving of information.

The opposite of high energy is obviously low energy. The price of low energy is usually determined by the reception we receive from others whom we would like to be responsive to our ideas.

Persuasion. Persuasion deals mostly with language and verbal skills. When combined with energy, the factor of body language also plays an important role.

How effective are you in getting other people to respond to your ideas—to buy into new methods, products, and services; to enjoy themselves in their business or personal environment; and to voluntarily spend more time with you?

Optimism. Optimism is an attitude created by a personal decision. The subconscious mind does not know the difference between the real or the imagined. You can imagine yourself healthy, happy, upbeat, and positive, or the opposite.

Optimism enables individuals to thrive in an otherwise negative environment, and by virtue of their optimism become a conduit for change within and to the environment.

Discipline. Discipline level can be measured by how frequently and effectively one approaches and completes those tasks that he doesn't really like to do. Discipline is a commitment to a way of life. It includes the planning of a business or a personal strategy, and the routine implementation of that strategy.

Each of the four elements interconnect with one another. In Chapter 1 we'll explore the energy component. In Chapters 2, 3, and 4 we'll continue with persuasion, optimism, and discipline, and discuss their interaction. Then we'll examine how the EPOD Theory can be applied to the array of situations you face, such as recruiting and supervising an effective staff, retaining professional counsel, negotiating agreements, and handling customer service complaints.

A TOOL YOU CAN USE

While the EPOD Theory is an efficient tool for understanding and internalizing the components of a successful business, certainly there are subcomponents to these common denominators. For example, enthusiasm and vigor support high energy. Stamina supports both high energy and discipline, and one can increase one's stamina through discipline. The four elements are sufficiently broad however, and overlap just enough, to help explain how success can be achieved.

The EPOD elements are not elaborate or exotic; they are within your grasp each day. While we live in a era that is becoming increasingly complicated, the EPOD elements are simple and they work. How many people are capable of reading and understanding a book entitled *The Arabic Notation of Integers*? The answer is practically everyone—we use the Arabic numerical system. Call the book *Basic Arithmetic*, and no one will be frightened. To achieve success, avoid overcomplicating matters—use a simple approach such as the EPOD Theory.

The EPOD Theory can be applied to all manner of human interaction, and everyone can benefit from it. Whether you are a teenager or senior citizen, the option of using it is always available, and it helps explain for example, why some seniors exhibit more energy than people half their age—transmitting energy is not as physiological as we are taught to believe.

THE EPOD ELEMENTS ARE INTER-RELATED

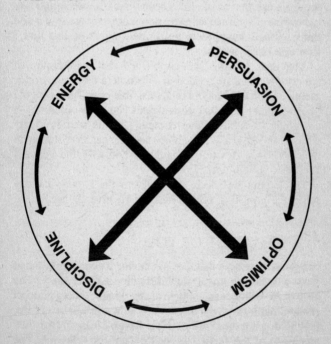

AS YOU THINK AND SPEAK

"But, Dave, I have no get-up-and-go. Maybe I could have more energy in my life, but I just don't see how."

Whatever you say, and whatever you feel, is going to affirm how you are. If you say, "I would like to learn how to apply the EPOD elements, but I don't have the time," then you will not have the time.

Though we are surrounded by role models who embody the traits we would like to exhibit, our own language and thoughts can prevent us from becoming who we would like to become. If you see an energetic or charismatic leader and think, "He is impressive, but I could never be like that," then you never will be.

Abundant research has established that a minimum of twenty-one days are needed to substitute a new behavior or practice in place of an old or undesirable one. The next time you encounter someone who inspires you, why not think, "I am going to exhibit more energy." If this sounds overly simple, try it; make the choice and repeat that statement over and over for twenty-one days. You will find yourself becoming a high-energy person.

Throughout this book, I'll refer to the twenty-one-day principle in making suggestions for positive change.

THE BEST OF YOU

People often tell me that they are having a good day or a bad day—a message that I find difficult to understand. The chemicals inside you, which create kinetic energy, don't change that much from day to day. When people say, "I'm feeling down today," they simple haven't learned that they manufacture the feeling of being "up" or "down." The perception is your option.

How you feel may be influenced by what you eat, what your are exposed to, and how late you got to bed last night, but your decision about how you are going to feel ultimately controls the way you will feel.

WHAT HAVE YOU DECIDED ABOUT TODAY?

In the computer industry there is a phrase GIGO ("garbage in garbage out"): whatever you put in the computer is what comes out. What are you putting into your personal information processor? That today is going to be a great day, or a disaster?

I am frequently asked if I experienced travel pressures in making 140 speeches a year. Often, I wake up in a hotel room wondering where I am, concerned about how I'll function for the rest of the day. Some of the day's developments may not be in my favor—the weather may turn foul, my flight may be delayed, I may be lacking some items that support my efforts. However, I do know that how I perceive the day is my choice. So, the moment I awake, the first thing I do is say my start-up statement out loud: "This is going to be a great day." This statement is an affirmation: it affirms or reinforces how I want to perceive the day.

Throughout the book I will discuss affirmations and how you can develop them to support how you want to feel. If the average individual would start each day with a personal affirmation, several positive developments would occur: There would be less chance of depression, fewer arguments and breakdowns in business relationships, and less need for external stimulants—alcohol, coffee, sugar, valium, marijuana, and other drugs—to create "feel good"s.

USING THIS BOOK

When you read a self-help book but don't take one important action, where is the real benefit? What are you going to
get from this book?

Anytime you flip through a book you see a passage that
interests you, immediately copy that page or clip the
appropriate passage and take action.

I collect copied passages from the books I read, tape them
to three-by-five cards, and file them. Periodically, I review
the file to see if any passages apply at the moment.

To stay abreast of what you need or what to know, have
people preread for you. Do you accumulate piles of materials you would like to read but never will? Are you
swamped? A secretary, assistant, husband, wife, child,
relative—almost anyone who can read—can become a
prereader for you.

I give my prereaders key words and themes that interest
me. I reply upon their judgment to highlight and underscore
those articles and passages that I would choose. This
doesn't stop me from reading other things that they may not
have highlighted.

Read with a highlighter. When you finish a book, no one
else should want it. Mark up your books, fold the pages,
and insert clips and notes throughout: use any tool that helps
you get the most from the book. Many people prefer to keep
their books in their original condition. But what is the
purpose of most nonfiction books? Usually it is to convey
information.

Start wherever you'd like. If you find it difficult to start
and stay with a book, open to the index or scan the pages
and read whatever interests you. Proceed backward, then

forward if you like; you don't have to submit to the tyranny of sequential page progression.

CASE HISTORIES

Dozens of actual case histories are used throughout this book to illustrate and emphasize points. The majority of cases and examples are based on personal experiences or observations. When possible, I have identified the individual or corporation by name, with permission. In some cases, however, to avoid embarrassment or revealing confidential details, names or other identification have been altered.

Having introduced the EPOD Theory and provided some suggestions for getting the most out of this book, let's focus on the energy element.

1 Energy!

A customer sees or hears your advertisement for something of which he may not have been aware. Your ads may say something like the following: "Come on in." "Come see us." "We want your business." "We have a great price." "We have great terms." "We have what you want." "This is a great place to do business."

Bolstered by stimulating messages, the customer visits your store, showroom, or model display in a high energy state. He or she invests time and effort in stopping by. Up to this point you've done everything right to capture the customer's attention.

Now, the $64,000 question: Will the same level of energy, excitement, and enthusiasm that the customer felt when first learning about your product or service be maintained when he or she actually visits and interacts with your employees? The answer to this question is always determined by your business environment.

To transmit high energy to another individual, give them the intensity of your full concentration.

Businesses make considerable efforts to improve product quality, ad copy, and interior design. Yes, these things are important, but they are not the fundamental reasons why customers keep coming back over the long term. These trappings don't mean a thing if they exist in a vacuum of low energy. The high price of low energy translates into low sales.

THE ILLUSION OF A HIGH-ENERGY ENVIRONMENT

Let's look a situation in which everything seems to be high energy, but in reality low energy is being transmitted to the customer.

You walk into a department store. You came because of an advertisement or a friend's recommendation, or perhaps the large sign caught your eye as you passed by. The showroom is dazzling—the carpeting is beautiful, the wall-covering exquisite, and all the windows spotlessly clean. So far, this business lives up to your expectations and transmits the message that you made a good choice in coming by. At this moment, you have high energy.

Initially, no one greets you, but you figure that's okay, business is great, and they probably have many things to take care of. Finally, someone emerges and utters the classic service question, "May I help you?"

The overwhelming majority of people respond, "No thanks, just looking." The energy level drops, and the impression of being in a special place dissipates. Why? As commonly spoken, the phrase "May I help you?" has been so overused that it is no longer perceived by the customer as a desire to help; it is received by many as an automatic, mundane, even trite, greeting. It is unimaginative and certainly nonaffirming.

When I say to you, "May I help you," the right side of your brain is not stimulated. You suspect that I am not really going to help you. I contribute to a situation in which you may leave sooner than you would have otherwise. The same phenomenon occurs if you call by phone and a voice answers, "XYZ and Company, may I help you?"

When you appeal to another person enthusiastically, romantically, musically, lyrically, passionately, you stimulate the right side of his brain. The left side of the brain, alternatively, is stimulated by logic, reasoning, practicality, and data.

How can you greet customers and impart high energy? How do I get you to stay in my store longer? By offering you an affirmation: "Thank you for coming in today," "I appreciate your coming in today," or "We are happy to have you here today." You don't often hear these kinds of greetings. When I offer these phrases, I am stimulating the right side of your brain and am making you feel better about the environment you are in. The chances are you are going to stay longer.

When you call my company, we say, "Thank you for calling Dave Yoho Associates." The words "thank you" are an expression of gratitude. They stimulate feelings of well-being and help develop harmonious relationships.

Even if the customer is skeptical about these different greetings, the power of the affirmations results in his overall feeling of well-being and increases the probability that he'll want to stay longer.

A BUSINESS THAT TRANSMITS HIGH ENERGY

Consider how customers feel when entering a Wal-Mart Store. They are enthusiastically welcomed with one of several responses: "Good Morning. Thank you for shopping Wal-Mart!" "Thanks for visiting Wal-Mart!" "Thank you for shopping Wal-Mart! My name is Joan." "Hi. We're glad to see you! Thank you for shopping Wal-Mart." "Good afternoon! We're glad you stopped in."

In all, a Wal-Mart host or hostess may offer the customer

about a dozen different greetings—but a lame "May I help you?" *is not one of them.*

Wal-Mart customers are greeted within thirty seconds of entering a store, even if all sales staff are presently helping customers. If this is the case, salespeople excuse themselves momentarily by asking customers whom they are currently serving, "Would you mind if I take a few moments to tell this person I will be with them shortly?" This question gains virtually 100 percent affirmative responses.

Temporarily freed, the salesperson uses one of the approved greetings with the new customer and then adds, "Thank you for your patience. Someone will be with you shortly." Both the initial customer and the one just entering feel important and satisfied—and maintain high energy levels.

Does Wal-Mart's high energy approach pay off? Ten years ago the nation's largest retailers were (1) Sears, (2) Montgomery Ward, and (3) JC Penney. Today, Sears is still the largest retailer in the world, followed by K Mart, then Wal-Mart. However, Wal-Mart operates in only twenty-nine states and has yet to benefit from the synergy of having a presence in all fifty, national advertising, and a national image. Yet, on a store-by-store basis, it frequently attains greater sales per square foot, sales per outlet, and average purchases per customer visit than Sears. For the thirteen years ending in January 1990, the Bentonville, Arkansas, discount chain raised its annual sales from $678 million to $26 billion.

A *New York Times* business journalist described Wal-Mart as "The most dramatically successful retail company in the last 20 years." A retail analyst for Smith, Barney, Harris, Upham and Company observed that "By the early 1990s Wal-Mart could exceed the sales of Sears or K Mart and it doesn't have to go national to do it." A retail analyst for Oppenheimer and Company said the company's growth rate is "one of the highest and its performance one of the most consistent in any economic environment."

Sam Walton, the company's founder, has been described as spreading equal parts of enthusiasm, evangelical spirit, and down-home glee to his more than two hundred thousand employees, who in turn transmit these to customers.

The difference is in the level of energy that Wal-Mart employees transmit to the customers. Throughout the company, Wal-Mart transmits high energy.

BEYOND CUSTOMER GREETINGS

Effective customer greetings are important in transferring energy, but they are not the whole story. While customers are at your place of business, each time they call, and any other interactions they have with you represent opportunities to convey high energy.

"NORDSTROM'S WITH A SONG." Walk into any outlet of Nordstrom's and you may immediately be struck by the excellent decor, the marble floors, the wide and inviting aisles, and the high-quality merchandise displays. But what sets Nordstrom's apart from their competitors is the soft piano music they provide for their customers.

You may not realize that you're hearing live, not canned, music. Each Nordstrom's outlet employs a tuxedo-clad piano player, and your right brain loves it. The store has been designed so that the music can be heard on all floors. You can be present for that music and never consciously know that you are being stimulated. Add Nordstrom's cheery salespeople, and you have an environment in which you are likely to stay a little longer than average.

What happens at Nordstrom's while you are standing around waiting for your companion to try on a product? They bring out a chair for you, and they look after your packages. Nordstrom's employees are taught to extend to you the same hospitality that you receive when invited into someone's home. This contributes to your feeling of well-being, and you want to stay longer.

Shopping at Nordstrom's is not perceived as a chore but as a pleasant experience. As such, the chances are you will want to buy something while you are there.

CASE #88: THE BANKING ENCOUNTER

You visit your bank. The decor is fabulous. Muzak plays softly in the background. You stand in line and are served by a teller in a reasonable amount of time. Your mission is to get a check cashed, so the bank can hardly disappoint you or reduce your energy level, right? Wrong!

You greet the teller and say, "I'd like to cash this check." The teller barely looks up—you are the seventy-eighth person he has seen today and it shows. He takes your check and identification, and runs through a series of verifications; that's okay, banks have to protect themselves.

For a moment you feel as if the teller is going to ask you for more identification or say that your check cannot be cashed. Maybe you're lucky and immediately he counts out the money. "Fifty, sixty, seventy, seventy-five dollars." Faster than your eyes can follow, he counts and hands you the cash. Then he bids you a nearly inaudible farewell. You leave the bank happy to have the cash, and relieved to be outside again. The bank environment is stifling, but you're not sure why. The answer: low energy.

Low energy responses convey to others that you do not care about them or see them as important. It conveys to customers that you don't attach significance to their presence at your place of business. Often, customers themselves are not actively aware when they are in a low energy environment. They do perceive that other business environments exist where they feel wanted, supported, and important.

Ultimately customers gravitate to companies with high-energy environments.

YOU MAY HAVE HIGH ENERGY,
BUT ARE YOU PASSING IT ON?

Most supervisors receive training in developing an effective staff. Many supervisors are proficient in personally maintaining high energy. Why, then, are they tolerant, or ignorant, of the low energy some of their staff members transmit to customers?

I asked a client who owned several fast-food franchises. "How many people work for you?" His reply was, "About half of them." The eighteen-year-old part-time counter person may be the type of person who naturally exudes high energy to customers. If so, it's a blessing for everyone. It is impractical to assume, however, that anyone at any age will automatically transmit high energy—the kind resulting in long-term customer patronage—without the proper training, and follow-up, and without a manager as an effective role model.

Sometimes low-energy people are promoted to managerial positions. Since their low energy is "endorsed" by promotion, they pass it on.

A poorly trained, fast-food counter person transmitting low energy all day gives hundreds of customers a poor impression of a particular franchise. Months pass and the counter person leaves. The franchise manager barely remembers the individual; so many are hired in the course of a year. Yet, to customers who received the low-energy transmission, that now-departed counter person *is* the Roy Rogers or the Burger King franchise.

It doesn't matter what else the manager does to ensure efficient operations—when those same customers patronize a competitor and receive a high-energy greeting and level of service, that is where they will return, though not necessarily knowing precisely why.

THE MOST IMPORTANT THINGS IN LIFE AREN'T THINGS

To transmit high energy to your staff, show them that you care about them, listen to them, greet them with high energy. The energy then transmitted to the staff is passed on to others they encounter. High energy can be conveyed softly and quietly, without clamor. To transmit high energy, acknowledge each person as a unique individual with special wants and needs.

The level of energy you transmit to another is not dependent upon your age, sex, ethnic origin, education, or experience. It is based upon the way you feel about yourself, your business, and the people you serve.

People are more important than products. If you are interested in maintaining an atmosphere in which motivation can occur, direct your energy toward your staff and they will take care of the product.

HIGH ENERGY IS ELECTIVE

On any given day, at any given moment, you can choose to transmit high energy. Here's a sales rep heading to work. Guess how much energy he will be transmitting to customers.

On the way to work this morning he feels great. It's May, the birds are singing, his family is doing fine; it is going to be a good day. Yesterday he closed a big sale, and he is looking forward to a big commission check at the end of the week.

Then he gets stopped by a traffic cop and is handed a twenty-five dollar ticket. Minutes later he gets a flat tire and is sidelined along the shoulder for thirty-five minutes.

When he does get to his office, his sales manager hands him a note that says yesterday's sale was cancelled because the customer's credit was not approved.

The first prospective customer he sees is abrasive and condescending. The salesman is verbally attacked several times in the span of about eight minutes. He is thankful when this prospect leaves.

The question is, what amount of energy will he transmit for the rest of the day? The answer: the level he chooses, or is assisted in developing by a high-energy manager. Of the next dozen people he sees, he might sell three of them; he's done it before. Or he could conclude that the whole day is shot, and simply go through the motions of interacting with prospects.

The energy that he transmits to others is totally a function of his internal decision-making process and/or how he is directed and stimulated in that environment. If he recognizes that a high energy level is in the customers' best interest and in his best interest, the traffic ticket, the flat tire, the lost sale, and the abrasive prospect will all have little effect on how he interacts with the next prospect.

YOUR LIFE ENERGY FORCE: MAINTAINING A HIGH ENERGY LEVEL

You know when you are feeling up—it's unmistakable. As a human being, however, you certainly can be influenced by external factors. What you may not realize is that almost every element to which we are exposed—foods, colors, other people, language, news—can effect us positively or negatively. We can't proceed through our day, however, waiting for or only seeking positive stimulation in order to stay positive. In waiting, the positive influences may come too intermittently or may not come at all.

Many people use anticipation to stay positive, but this

often boomerangs. Suppose you have been invited to what you know will be a fabulous party. You're up. ("I am really looking forward to this party.") You are experiencing a stimulated high. What happens once that party is over? You will probably equally experience a low. Possibly you will depend on outside stimulation or other forces to make you feel good again.

Would you like to maintain a fairly even, consistent high? It is possible to do this through positive thought, affirmations, and choice.

CASE #17: YOUR THOUGHTS INFLUENCE YOUR LEVEL OF ENERGY

The marine colonel who stood in front of me was about six-foot-three, and I estimated his weight at about 250 pounds. He looked like a weight lifter or professional athlete. He was a volunteer from the audience I was addressing on Dr. John Diamond's research and findings in behavioral kinesiology (BK), and how this affects one's amount of energy, as indicated through muscle testing.

I explained to the audience that as long as you're alive, you have a life energy force. It is affected by many things in your environment, such as food, clothes, art, poetry, and music. While it's your decision to transmit high energy or not, there are factors that add to your energy and others that can diminish it. For example, a negative thought or idea can at least temporarily diminish your energy.

Now I was going to have to prove it, using the obviously skeptical colonel. I put him through a basic BK muscle test.

"Stick out your left arm at the shoulder," I said, facing him from about two feet away. He did. His arm looked as if I could have swung from it. I told him that I could actually deplete his physical strength with a negative thought. This drew snickers from the audience and a smile from the colonel.

First, I gave him a positive message. Grasping his outstretched arm, I said, "Colonel, you seem to be an officer we can be proud of him. You are obviously a man of authority, a man with command presence, a strong leader." I tried to push down on his arm, but it would not budge.

He was pleased at my failed attempt to bring his arm down. Then, in a serious tone, I told him something that was completely untrue: "But, there's a problem here. Did you know that scientific research has proven that on the average, career military people are less intelligent than the general population?" Then I pushed down on his arm again, exerting the same pressure as before. His arm muscles weakened, and I was able to bring the colonel's arm down instantly. His jaw dropped just as fast, and the onlookers were dumbfounded.

SKEPTICS BECOME BELIEVERS

I have re-enacted that demonstration hundreds of times in corporate boardrooms and in training seminars. The results are always the same. The skeptics remain skeptics until they go through or witness the second half of the demonstration, when I give a negative suggestion.

I had long believed in the strong connection between feelings of well-being and high personal performance. When I learned about Dr. John Diamond's book, *BK* Behaviorial Kinesiology: The New Science for Positive Health Through Muscle Testing*, and his work in the field of behavioral kinesiology, I was able to make scientific sense of what I already knew practically.

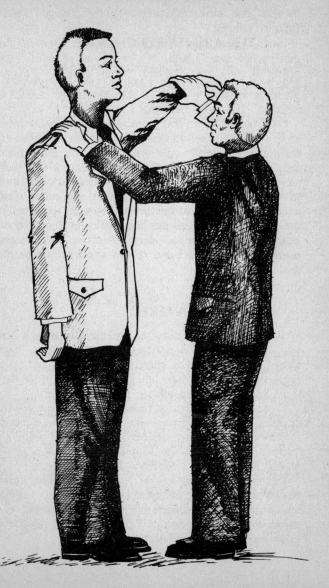

THE ABILITY TO CHOOSE

When I uttered false, negative statements to the colonel, I temporarily weakened him. Through positive affirmations, silently reviewed, it would be possible for the colonel to resist my push, no matter what I said.

Psychiatrist Viktor Frankl, a World War II concentration-camp survivor, observed that the people who survived the death camps were the ones who consciously and deliberately chose how they would be *in* the camp. Their basic secret was that although their bodies were in captivity, their spirits were not. They could choose their own attitudes and remain free in the most fundamental sense of the term.

Dr. Frankl concludes that this ability to choose one's attitudes enabled him and others to survive while others, many of whom were better treated and in better health, died.

BEING CENTERED

When a subject is unaffected by the BK muscle test following a negative suggestion, it is called being "centered." The individual's energies are centered and he is invulnerable to stress. Remaining centered most of the time is an obtainable and appropriate goal for each of us.

Those who concentrate on their own self-worth instead of doubting themselves or wallowing in self-pity, who choose to see beauty instead of ugliness, who respond positively instead of negatively, are happier and more productive people, and maintain a consistent life energy force.

This is not an original insight. In many ways, what I have just written is a cliché of human behavior. Perhaps for that reason millions of people scoff at the idea that you can choose to have higher energy. Still, even among those who know the facts, many refuse to act on them.

PERSONAL ENERGY AFFECTS HOW WE LIVE

Dr. Diamond makes the observation that if you stand at a busy street corner in any city and watch people walk by, "most of these people seem like prisoners on the earth," rather than vibrant creatures, full of joy and glad to be alive.

Factors that lower body energy include overly refined and unnatural foods, poor air quality, noise pollution, and synthetic fabrics, as well as characteristics of the individual, including posture, the ability to handle stress, and negative thoughts or suggestions.

Factors that tend to increase body energy include positive thoughts, good nutrition, fresh air, pleasant sounds and surroundings, natural fibers, and, indeed, most things natural.

Take a look at your business or personal environment. Identify the conditions that might lead to low energy and decide which of them can be corrected immediately, and which require short- or long-range strategies for correction.

THE NUTRITION-ENERGY LINK

The average American living to the age of seventy will consume approximately one hundred thousand pounds of food and twelve to fifteen pounds of medicine. Every time the food contributes to a set of conditions that makes him or her ill, the individual seeks out a new medicine rather than be denied the luxury of the offending food.

Most of the breads, meats, and poultry, and other food items found in supermarkets today are laced with preservatives and other chemicals, largely for the benefit (profitability, and so on) of the grower, processor, manufacturer, or seller. Seldom do any of these preservatives lead to a consumer benefit.

Medical science has made enormous health advances in the last several decades, including laser surgery, organ transplants, and miracle vaccines. Yet these advances have been counterbalanced by the medical community's inability to make public the fact that a poor or unbalanced diet is the principle cause of most illnesses and energy deficiencies.

CASE #49: FROM LOW MORALE TO HIGHER ENERGY

Earl Windom, a senior vice president at a corporation with sales in excess of $1 billion, was experiencing a morale problem as an aftermath of his company being acquired by a major U.S. corporation. My company was brought in to analyze production, restaffing procedures, and sagging profits.

Low energy was a symptom of many conditions in the company's environment. By analyzing the following conditions and instituting rapid changes, we initiated a swift turnaround.

An adversarial attitude existed between the engineering and marketing departments, which led to a slowdown in the work flow and constant bickering between department heads, who were supposed to be working cooperatively. A joint conference was held, at which an experiment was proposed to eliminate the following three conditions from phone language: value-judging words such as should, ought, and must; adversarial language (more *we* and less *you* versus *me*); the tendency to respond to anger, hostility, and belligerence in kind, instead of with an affirmation of understanding. The process took effect in approximately forty-five days. Within ninety days the measurable energy level had risen.

Managers working in windowless cubicles experienced low energy toward the end of eight- or ten-hour days. White fluorescent bulbs were changed to "full spectrum" bulbs, which imitate sunlight, and the managers experienced increased energy functioning in the same offices.

Morning staff meetings were accompanied by coffee and danish. We convinced management to serve natural fruit juices, fruit, and low-sodium, sugarless breads and crackers. There was quite a transition problem here. The taste buds get used to elements (sugar, salt, caffeine) that reduces bodily energy. However, within two months, 60 percent of the participants had adopted the natural foods.

A high level of negative language was directed toward the new parent company, flowing to line workers and low-entry positions, and ultimately to customers, vendors, and others. We held a series of seminars demonstrating through muscle testing how low energy is created by negativity, and convincing the participants that they were the first to suffer, not the other employees, customers, or vendors. A contract was negotiated with all employees, asking them to refrain from negative language for ninety days and to reconvene at that time for reevaluation and measuring. Ninety-two percent of the employees at these seminars negotiated the contract. More than sixty percent stayed with the program for ninety days. The result of the program was that employees were able to cut down on the amount of negative language.

The positive, as well as negative, factors affecting individuals within any environment can be simply measured through the BK muscle test. Once these factors are identified and understood by those affected, effective solutions can be readily introduced.

LEFT AND RIGHT BRAIN THINKING

Left and right brain thinking influence the life energy force. Typically the left brain is the location of the language center and is the hemisphere that specializes in logical, analytical, mathematical processing. It is where rational, factual thinking takes place. Other parts of the left brain specialize in linear, sequential, detailed modes of thinking that are used in planning, organizing, and administrative processing.

The right brain generally is the center of intuitive and insightful thinking, where we can process information simultaneously and where conceptual thinking can take place. It is the location of our ability to synthesize as opposed to analyze. The right hemisphere also deals with specialized areas of interpersonal processing, emotional thinking, and music appreciation. It is where we recognize faces as opposed to names, and it is where we do our nonverbal thinking.

We make decisions in the definitive sense with the right side of the brain, although we weigh the various factors and arrive at our decision in the left side of the brain.

CHARACTERISTICS OF LEFT AND RIGHT BRAIN THINKING

Left	Right
Analytical and objective	Artistic and innovative, subjective
Regards time as continuous and sequential	Regards time as a series of discrete snapshots of past, present, and future
Recognizes conceptual similarities but not spatial ones	Recognizes spatial similarities but not conceptual ones
Verbal expression	Nonverbal expression, gestures, limited word usage
Understands through building basic concepts	Understands through perception, image building

Limited intake of detail	Nearly unlimited intake of detail, because of image-building capability

How can you achieve hemispheric balance? Reading an ordinary newspaper lowers your energy, as do reports and technical data, while looking at most brightly colored paintings raises energy. People who take energy breaks during the day, who stop and recite an affirmation or the verse of a favorite poem, or look at a favorite picture or painting, greatly reduce their stress and help themselves move toward balance.

Our immediate physical environment has a dramatic impact on our energy.

LOVE YIELDS HIGH ENERGY

The most intriguing of Dr. Diamond's findings for me was how the emotional state increases or decreases life energy. Diamond found that feelings of love, faith, trust, encouragement, and gratitude were deep emotions that stimulated and, in general, strengthened individuals. Conversely, feelings of hate, suspicion, fear, and resentment fostered weakness and imbalance.

"I am absolutely convinced," says eminent physician and author Dr. Bernie Siegel, "that the feeling of support I grew up with gave me the belief that I could be what I wanted to be and guided me toward my desire to give and to heal."

IMPLEMENTING A BK REGIMEN

Implementing a BK regimen in business is simple. Nevertheless, I find I have to proceed cautiously because the client employees may perceive BK testing as a trick or gimmick. Yet if I can convince them to observe the impact of high energy on themselves, peers, and customers, they buy into the idea and slowly, but surely, high energy becomes a way of life.

SUPPORTING A HIGH-ENERGY WORK ENVIRONMENT: REPLACEMENT/SUPPLEMENT TECHNIQUES

Low Energy	High Energy	Strategy
Hard rock music (most)	Classical Modern Jazz Some country/western	Piped-in music
Sugar	Honey	Dispenser in commisary, kitchenettes
Fast food	Fruits, nuts, grains	Coffee breaks Lunch breaks Meetings and conferences
Smoking (presence of)	Nonsmoking environment	Restricted areas, policy
Criticism	Acknowledgment Assessment Observation data	Change methods of review
Value judging (should, ought, must)	Nonjudgmental language	Behavior modification
Left brain stimulation (logic, practicality, technical data)	Right brain stimulation (enthusiasm, emotion)	Appeal to both Seek balance

DETERMINING YOUR OWN ENERGY LEVEL

The following quiz will help you gauge how you currently apply energy.

HOW MUCH ENERGY DO I BRING TO WHAT I DO?

Points: [0]   [1]   [2]   [3]
       Never   Occasionally   Frequently   Always

1. Do I activate my energy system or do I wait for others or outside circumstances to bring me a "feel good"?
2. Do I transmit enthusiasm in my voice when I greet others and answer the phone?
3. Do I reflect high energy in my eye-to-eye contact and handshake?
4. Do I use gestures and body movements when I am explaining or selling to others?
5. Do I hum, sing, or recite in my shower and when alone in my car?
6. Do I exhibit undivided interest in the conversation of others?
7. Do I maintain a balance—neither a comedian nor a grouch; friendly yet not overly intimate?
8. Do I *not* permit setbacks or disappointments to reduce my energy on a daily basis?
9. Do I avoid the "blahs" early in the day that influence my production and interpersonal relationships later?
10. Do I laugh spontaneously?

If you scored under 25, the energy that you transmit is *not sufficient* to ensure that your staff, customers, and business environment reverberate with an energy level sufficient for success. Your goal is to consistently score 25 or higher.

The best way to increase your score is to copy the questions for which your score is low and prominently post them on your bathroom mirror, near your desk, or wherever convenient. For the next twenty-one days, simply read them each morning. Then, take the test again; your new score may surprise you.

YOU'RE IN CHARGE

When you give high energy, you get high energy. When you pick up that phone and enthusiastically greet callers, you get more enthusiastic responses. When giving your spouse a big hug, you tend to get it back. The key is to stimulate your feelings of well-being before you address someone. At seminars, I tell people who use the telephone, "Smile before you dial."

You can control your energy level, health, environment, and destiny; the key ingredient is—you.

EPOD TACTICS

• Don't depend on others for your "feel goods." Manufacture them each day through personal affirmations.

• How is the phone answered in your company? When the phone rings in your office, do your receptionists say, "ABC Company, will you hold?" and then immediately put callers on hold? Thirty seconds on hold can seem like an eternity.

"On hold" means "ignore." Ray Johnson, former CEO of Coachmen Industries, realizing how insidious the hold button can be, relabeled all the hold buttons in his office to read "IGNORE." This gave his employees a continual reminder that every time they placed a caller on hold, they were actually ignoring that caller.

• To transmit a high level of energy to others, give them your undivided attention, listen to them intently, as if nothing else exists. If a customer on the phone with your service department perceives that your representative's attention is divided, then the customer receives low energy.

• Put yourself in the company of positive, high-energy people.

• The traditional corporation operates on left-brain thinking, utilizing logic, empirical data, statistics, systematized procedures, and a tightly structured organizational chart.

The traditional entrepreneur often concentrates in the right-brain direction, inclusive of large doses of creativity, rapid changes, rugged individualism, being reactive, and rejecting old ways and methods.

The two concepts seem almost irreconcilable yet when there is a balance of right- and left-brain thinking and a permission for each to exist at every level of the business, a dynamic organization emerges.

• Test yourself; your body doesn't lie. You do not need to rely on someone else's opinion as to how something will affect you. You can become your own energy advisor.

• Follow the BK dictum: "Choose those things for which you test strong; avoid those things with which you test weak."

• Take frequent energy breaks, reciting your affirmations, particularly upon waking and during stressful situations.

• Listen to revitalizing music or positive attitude tapes.

• Concentrate on pleasant thoughts and positive images of yourself and others.

• Hug your spouse, children, companions.

• Practice smiling.

• Think, walk, and act with high energy.

• Dwell on positive thoughts such as love, faith, trust, gratitude, and courage.

• Practice high-energy techniques daily to continually raise your life's energy and positively affect those around you.

2 Persuasion

Customer satisfaction is a
perception.
            —Dave Yoho

John sat with his head in his hands. For the fourth
time that afternoon, he had given his all to a customer only
to have the customer leave, saying, "Let me get back to
you" or "I need to think it over." John carefully contem-
plated each encounter. As far as he could determine, he was
totally responsive to customer questions and concerns.

He greeted each customer cheerfully, asking, "How are
you today?" Any time a customer asked John if his
department carried a product, John was quick to point out
the extensive selection available. John knew that he had the
products to satisfy customers, but for some reason he was
not persuasive.

The reason? John had high energy, but he wasn't using
power words (words that influence, encourage, or affirm).
When a customer asked a question, John was quick to
respond with the answer, but good communication and
persuasive language call for *answering a question with
another question*, to better understand and show interest in
someone. This is particularly true in selling.

REMOVING THE BLOCKS TO MORE PERSUASIVE LANGUAGE

Your language and the way you use it determines your ability to persuade. I've found that many words and phrases, because of misuse and overuse, are not persuasive; instead they tend to neutralize otherwise effective interaction. Overused words, such as personal references (I, me, my) and meaningless adjectives (fantastic, fabulous), are often neutralizers or turn-offs.

Questions that halfheartedly ask about one's health ("How are you feeling?") or statements that direct one ("You really should try this.") have about the same effect as "May I help you?"—they transmit low energy to others; hence they attract low energy. Here's a brief list of unpersuasive language:

Fabulous	This is the truth.
Brand new	Do you follow me?
Unbelievable	May I help you?
I, we, me, our	How are you today?
Out of this world	Sign this.
Really	What's up?
Between you and me	You should, ought, or must

Now measure the extent and way in which this language is used both by you and your acquaintances.

In contrast, the following words and phrases have power; they affirm or acknowledge others. Most readers are familiar with all of these, yet they use them infrequently in their interactions.

Economy	Protection	Profitable	You, your
Unexcelled	Experience	Dependable	Share
Assurance	Genuine	Pride	Help
Enjoyment	Expert	Security	Money
Quality	Popular	Convenience	Save
Prestige	Confidence	Peace of mind	New
Service	Efficient	Original	Love
Courtesy	Durable	Fun	Results
Growth	Reputation	Stimulating	Easy
Relief	Necessary	Modern	Proven
Stylish	Successful	Health	Guarantee
Thank you for	I appreciate	I understand	Discovery

Some of these words reflect feelings, while others offer believable promises of safety, security, fun, happiness, and solutions to problems.

To effectively use more powerful words and to measure their effects, select and circle three from above. Use them in your language for the next twenty-one days, then select three more, and repeat the process.

Persuasion is the art of using language to ensure that an individual's experience is pleasant and comfortable enough that the individual will be willing to accept what you would like him or her to do within your environment. Energy and persuasion are closely linked. Without the appropriate energy, it is doubtful that you can be persuasive.

HEDGING LANGUAGE DOES LITTLE TO PERSUADE

Between neutral language and persuasive words and phrases comes hedging. Hedging phrases are those that mean little or nothing or those which disguise what one really thinks or feels, such as "You know best," "It doesn't make any difference," or "Whatever you decide is okay with me."

One of my favorite anecdotes provides an excellent illustration of hedging language that fails to persuade. It's about an Irish priest, during Holy Week, who has a heavy bias against the British.

On Friday, the priest gives his best sermon. He says to the congregation

This is the night that we celebrate the Last Supper. 'Twas at the Last Supper that Jesus spoke to the Apostles and said, "One of you will betray me."

And he looked at Peter and said, "Will it be you?" And Peter said, "No, it will not be me, Master."

He looked at James and said, "James, will it be you?" And James said, "No, it will not be me, Savior."

Then he looked at Judas and said, "Judas, will it be you?" And Judas said, "Look 'ere, Guv'nor . . ."

LANGUAGE THAT IS NOT PERSUASIVE

Being persuasive does not mean downgrading competitor products, ridiculing alternative approaches, or resorting to negative language of any kind. Persuasive language means eliminating the need for high-pressure or deceptive sales methods.

Unfortunately, our political system may be devolving to

the point where candidates are elected based on how effectively they are able to portray the other candidates as inept, rather than on how they will handle the critical issues of the day.

Attempts to be persuasive using negative language are detrimental to both the speaker and the listener.

CASE # 40: BUSINESS MEETS THE PRESS

Curt Jones, age thirty-eight, is newly assigned as general manager of a medium-sized division of a major corporation. His record of success is impressive, and he has a reputation for being tough, hardworking, and hard-nosed. He has brought several members of his team with him from the "other" division.

He received his new post because the division to which he has been assigned has been plagued by morale and production problems. It also has been drowning in red ink for two years. Curt's team focuses immediately on the problems. First, the assessment group evaluates personnel, then it evaluates the components of the business, such as production, purchasing, marketing, sales, and finance.

Next, Curt and his staff develop long- and short-range plans. They restructure the marketing plan, the operating system, and the organizational chart. They prepare a list of personnel changes, including managerial. Curt devises an orderly transition plan. All this is accomplished within seventy-five days.

Curt schedules a press conference to help ensure continuing industry and market base support, as well as condition the local community to the changes.

During the press conference, Curt is responsive to the questions regarding his background and the goals for this division. Several members of the press start to use "zinger"-type questions and negative reflections, but Curt is no stranger to this kind of interaction.

PRESS: Mr. Jones, we understand that your transition plan calls for furloughing 750 plant and middle management persons, is that correct?

CURT: That is correct.

        [Bravo, Curt, no speeches—just facts.]

PRESS: Have you considered the economic effect this will have on these people and this community?

CURT: Yes, we have, and we regret the need to make this kind of decision, but it's either that or shut down the plant and get out of this business.

[Here, Curt's tough management is showing through—it invites the press to pose the next question.]

PRESS: Do I understand that closing the plant and discontinuing the business was an option?

CURT: Obviously if a company is not making money with a product line, they would be wise to get out of the business quickly. We chose other alternatives.

[Tough again, Curt. The general statement about companies getting out of the business if they can't make a profit is good business logic. Hmm, I wonder if the press heard it that way?]

PRESS: Based on your background and success in the company's other divisions, I'm sure they have confidence in your plan. But suppose it doesn't work, or doesn't work as rapidly as anticipated? Could we expect to see more layoffs or even more drastic measures, such as the other option you mentioned?

CURT: Anything is possible; however, I'm reasonably certain that our proposed changes will be effective. It is our intent to keep a check on all facets of the business and the changes we have directed. We'll know soon if we are doing enough things right. I have asked my staff to evaluate our overall progress in 120 days.

[Curt, you are an action guy, it's obvious, and you are

sending out a message—give us results or more changes will follow.]

The press conference continues with this type of interaction. The reporters leave with a clear picture of Curt's tough style, assured that he is the kind of manager who can pull this company out of its financial morass, bring the plant back to the full operations it once enjoyed, and reinstate its positive economic impact on the community.

The next day, the business section of the largest local newspaper devotes the front page to Curt's press conference. It praises his tough style and his long-range plans. Consider, however, some of the highlighted statements: "New general manager says, 'We'll make a profit or shut down.'" "'We laid off 750 people—it's purely a business decision.'" "New general manager says he will reevaluate in 4 months." [Hold your breath.] "More layoffs could follow." "New GM says, 'I want results in 120 days or else.'"

Now evaluate the impact of the statements above, even though they have been printed out of context. Worker morale is affected—we all tend to react to what is in a newspaper, seldom assessing its validity. Those who face impending layoff, await further cuts, and aren't sure of where they stand are all affected by the newspaper's portrayal of tough management.

Those who have a relatively secure position with seniority or other special status detect in Curt's tough management stance the message "Either we make the necessary changes quickly to achieve profits, or we close down this company."

The product that this company manufactures is in a highly competitive field. Each employee's productivity is vital in keeping the company highly competitive. Stability, product availability, turnaround time, and follow-through service are major factors that affect market share.

Within two days of the article, the competitors' salespeople are armed with copies of it. With subtle references,

40 Dave Yoho and Jeffrey P. Davidson

innuendo, and mild distortions, they paint a vivid picture throughout the sales territories of the extremely tentative and shaky position of Curt's division.

THE PREPARATION TO BE PERSUASIVE

Curt did not use persuasive language, to the detriment of the company and himself. To prepare himself for such an event, he could have shared his presentation in advance with his key staff to better gauge the potential impact of his language. Curt could even have held a mock press conference to surface any issues that might be contentious. Also, he could have circulated a carefully worded statement, recognizing that the press often uses segments of prepared messages and transcripts.

To preempt some of the zinger-type questions, Curt could have developed and circulated a list of ten or twelve likely questions along with answers.

Because Curt did not undertake these exercises (a *discipline*—more in Chapter 4) the language that he used, and hence his overall persuasiveness, ultimately was ineffective. It would be hard to assess Curt as a poor general manager, yet by using unpersuasive language, he made a tough situation even tougher.

THE POTENTIAL IN EVERY ENCOUNTER

Persuasive language is certainly an effective tool to impress a new or first-time customer, but it is much more. It is a manner of speaking, using language, and responding that conveys the message "We are in business to serve you." Many companies today want to provide effective customer service. Yet the one-on-one capability to offer persuasive language that satisfies the customer's perception of service is often lacking in business.

Each time the phone rings or a new customer comes to your company, the potential exists for a sale and/or a long-term relationship. Each customer with a service request (or complaint) represents another opportunity for your business.

How do you say "Hello"? Companies that recognize the importance of using appropriate language actually write scripts for customer greetings and ensure that all employees use them. As Curt's experience illustrates, the use of persuasive language is too important to be left to chance.

At Dave Yoho Associates, how we greet customers and callers is so vital to our persuasiveness and hence the environment we choose to maintain, that we follow a script, which starts with the affirmation "Thank you for calling Dave Yoho Associates." People tell me, "Wow, that person who answers the phone for you sure does a good job." Other people tell me, "You've had the same receptionist for about five years, right?" Callers don't realize that it is not the same receptionist; it is just consistent, persuasive language.

Persuasive language offers a believable promise, much like good copy in a printed advertisement. Persuasive language means addressing the customer or prospect at his level of reception—not easy to do, since our society is egocentric: we think that sharing our experience of the world or of a product will persuade others. Our society also teaches first-party language: "I did this . . . ," "I did that . . ." "I want to show you . . . ," "I want to tell you . . ." "Our company . . . ," "Our group . . ." "Our method . . . ," "Our solution . . ."

The people you speak to listen based on their experience. The solution is to become more "other-centric" and to put more "you" and "your" into the language (at least at the start of your discussion) and less "I" and "our."

The first rule of sales presentations (oral or printed) is to start with the word "you" and "your."

WHAT THE CUSTOMER NEEDS, NOT WHAT YOU HAVE

When I ask for a workbench and you immediately reply, "We have all kinds here, so I think we can take care of you," you are *not* using persuasive language. Why? Because your focus is on what you have and not on what I need.

Your goal is to find out what I need, so that you can be persuasive. First, determine the key features I seek. Listening to what I say, you are in a far better position to offer a solution to my needs. Now you can offer what you have. And if you've done your job correctly, I will be more receptive to what you recommend (even though the solution to my needs may be the item you had in mind all along).

CREDENTIALS NOT REQUIRED—persuasion has nothing to do with credentials. The salesperson who talks about his or her latest success, education, background, experience, or the like is not employing persuasion. Persuasiveness is predicated on how receptive you are to another.

Increase your persuasiveness in general by learning as much about customers in general as possible and, in particular, by learning about the customer in front of you. To be persuasive, transmit the following within your message: "I care about you." "I care about what you are doing." "I want to understand you." "I want to understand your goal."

You then deliver a message that fits the customer's needs. Without resorting to egocentric language, it is helpful to convey that you face or have faced some of the same problems as the customer. You want to convey the message, "I come from the same place, and together we can solve your particular problem," be it a purchase or a service need.

The next time you go to buy a carpet, observe whether the salesperson asks: "How many people are in your home?" "How many children?" "What functions take place in this room?" "How long have you lived in this house?" "What kind of floor covering do you have now?"

This is persuasive language. The salesperson does the asking; the customer does the responding. The proper use of these questions indicates that the salesperson cares not just about making a sale, but also about providing a product or service that meets your needs and specifications.

PERSUASION IS THE KEY TO EFFECTIVE CUSTOMER SERVICE DEPARTMENTS

Effective, persuasive language is particularly important in the customer service (or complaint) department. In successful companies, the customer relations staff are taught that they are just as important to a company's persuasiveness in developing long-term customers as the front-line sales staff. They are also taught the following: Problems are what created their job. The customer is a necessary asset to a business. Calming an excited, demanding, or upset customer is a challenge, not a confrontation. The person with the greatest skill level usually ends up being in charge.

The issue is not who is right or who is wrong. The real issue is customer satisfaction. Effective customer relations reps learn that while customers may or may not be right, their feelings and perceptions are always important, and effective service is based solely on customer perception. Thus the statement "The customer is always right" is a perception.

Companies who train their service departments to respond to customers by expressing the message "Thank you for calling this to our attention" or "Please give me all the facts, and do you mind if from time to time I ask questions?" fare better in the long run, incur less customer dissatisfaction, and retain service representatives who feel good about their roles.

CASE #56; NO MALICE FROM ALICE

Alice Martin, a customer service representative in the auto parts department of a large metropolitan store, is skilled in using effective, persuasive language.

She receives a phone call from an irate customer who is seeking to exchange an expensive set of custom wheels; he's been back to the store twice already, and the latest set contains blemishes. While the customer is shouting and using vile language, Alice gets the necessary information to solve the problem.

The customer, growing more impatient, eventually explodes.

"Lady," he screams, "you can take these wheels and shove 'em up your . . ." The remarks were uncalled for and in bad taste, but Alice keeps her cool.

Calmly she replies, "Sir, I appreciate your offer, but I'm already dealing with a stereo radio and set of hubcaps that were directed to the same part of my anatomy yesterday." Then she pauses.

The customer cannot believe his ears. He pauses, asks her name, and within forty minutes is standing at her counter laughing. The wheels are exchanged and his problem is solved. Alice retains a customer for her company— perhaps for years—because of her persuasive, effective language skills.

HOW PERSUASIVE AM I?

Points: [0] [1] [2] [3]
Never Occasionally Frequently Always

1. Do I refrain from using first-person language (I, we, me) as opposed to second-person language (you, your, yours) in conversation with others?
2. Do I avoid stereotypical, low-persuasive greetings (e.g., "May I help you?") in place of more positive language?
3. Do I avoid cliché phrases such as "unbelievable," "awesome," "out of this world," "between you and me," "this is the truth," or "do you follow me?"
4. Do I avoid value-judging words and phrases such as "you should," "you ought to," "you must"?
5. Do I avoid using phrases that have become meaningless, such as "how are you today," "how are you feeling," or "how is the weather?"
6. Do I shun trying to win arguments at the risk of breaking down relationships?
7. Do I listen fully before I respond?
8. Do I avoid talking too much to convince others what I know?
9. Am I patient with the responses of others?
10. Do I avoid talking too much with those that seem more affable and attentive?

If your score is 15 or less, you require a serious revision of your interactive language. If your score is 18 or more, concentrate more on using power words and phrases. If your score is 23 or more, you are on the right track. With a score of 25 or more, simply keep doing what you are doing—you are being persuasive.

Remember, in areas where your score is low, simply posting the question over your desk and reading it for a minimum of twenty-one days will help you to improve your ability in that area—you will be conscious of your desire to improve.

EPOD TACTICS

• The first rule of sound communication and persuasive language is talk less, acknowledge more, and listen longer.
• Use affirming language on a regular basis.
• Include power words and phrases in your daily conversation.
• Ask questions.
• Every time you revisit a prospect or one comes into your place of business, include an appreciation phrase very early in the conversation: "I appreciate your time today." "I appreciate your continuing business." "I appreciate your seeing me today." "I appreciate the order recently received." "I appreciate your calling to my attention XYZ."
• To be truly persuasive means to convert confrontations into successful relationships.
• Pause four seconds before you respond to a complaint or an objection, and always respond with a question. It shows you care about what was said. It sets the tone for a response, and the response broadens your ability to understand the circumstances.
• Practice your upbeat, persuasive techniques in front of a mirror, on the phone, and with your family. In the latter case, you will get immediate feedback.
• Always start your memos and letters with a second-party reference other than a first-party reference (you, your as opposed to I, we, me). It's called writing for the reader and has automatic (yet unconscious) appeal to the recipient.
• 80 percent of your customers will respond to effective customer service. About 20 percent of your customer base

(we'll call them the A's) will continue to do business with you despite numerous inequities in your customer service.

Another 20 percent, the B's will not be satisfied no matter what you do if there is a minor breakdown or glitch. The remaining 60 percent of your customer base, the C's, can be influenced with better than average customer service techniques.

The A's and C's comprise 80 percent of your customer base and represent a strong reason to continually develop a customer service program.

3 Optimism

I met a man who was so optimistic he'd say,
"if I die," not "when I die."

—Dave Yoho

Optimism begets optimism. When you give high energy, you get high energy. If you pick up that phone and enthusiastically greet callers, you receive more enthusiastic responses. Optimism works the same way.

The key is to stimulate your feelings of well-being before you address someone.

Optimism is nothing more than an outlook generated by the brain. The mind does not know the difference between what is real and what is imagined. You bring optimism into your environment much as you bring energy—by choosing it. As optimism begets a positive response from others, pessimism begets a negative response from others.

Optimism is the ability to recognize that opportunities that await you may have no connection to anything that has come before. Optimism is a deep-down, chosen feeling that you can accomplish your goals.

OPTIMISM IS OPTIONAL

In almost any situation, you can choose optimism or pessimism. For example, let's say sales for a particular business haven't been up to par in the last year. The sales manager assembles her staff for a closed-door meeting. She begins by saying, "We have got to improve sales. Otherwise, we may not be in business by next year."

Suppose the same manager says, "We have a high potential to do a lot of business. While we are not meeting our goals now, I firmly believe we can in the future. We can do better because we are better." Which statement is likely to generate optimism and positive action on the part of the staff?

Following poor first-quarter sales, the wise manager takes an optimistic view about what can be done during the year's remaining three quarters. The pessimistic manager, consciously and subconsciously, prepares for a disastrous year. Her feeling is disseminated in one way or another to the employees and the customers. Sure enough, the company has a bad year.

You are in real estate sales. You think to yourself, "The mortgage market is down. This is probably the wrong time to be in this business. Why did I get myself into this situation?"

Now, contrast these thoughts with the following: "The mortgage market is down, and that's going to scare the hell out of a lot of people in this business. This is the time to be in the real estate business, because the weak ones aren't going to 'cut it.' The best sales will go to the tough cookies like me."

Another example: You sell cars for a living and you notice that everyone is buying the competitor's cars. You start thinking, "Theirs is a great car, but who wants to drive down the pike in the same car as everyone else? We have a great opportunity now to sell our cars."

A negative viewpoint could have been selected: "Theirs is the hottest selling car on the market. Yup, everyone's buying it. We can't compete with that car; half the people that come into our showroom ask me how our cars measure up to that one. I might as well fold up the tent; there's no use even trying to compete with it."

Optimism *is* optional.

CASE #18: TOGETHER WE CAN SUCCEED

Optimism in business involves decoding a set of facts and feeding it to another human being in a manner that prompts positive action. Persuasiveness and optimism are inextricably linked, as are energy and optimism.

Consider the optimism of Lee Iacocca at the height of Chrysler's difficulties. He was faced with a large and complex set of problems, among them financial insolvency, poor profitability, and low morale. Anyone who is familiar with Lee Iacocca's management style could not assess it as being soft. Given the circumstances he was facing, equivalent to reviving a bankrupt company, no one but a tough manager would have taken the job.

As one of the Chrysler dealers later related to me, Iacocca maintained an optimistic tone in a crucial policy change with the Chrysler dealers. He first stressed the dealers' importance to the corporation and explained how decisions changing policies would affect them. He emphasized their prominence in the corporate marketing structure. Then, to engender the dealers' support even more, he imparted a message something like this: "I know this is how we used to do it. However, we simply cannot continue the practice. [Chrysler's maintenance of a large automobile inventory to meet dealers' future needs, a costly and impractical system.] I need your cooperation in reducing this current inventory and in the transition to the 'you order it, we make it' philosophy. I know with your help we can make this the strong company it once was."

This is an example of a strong manager soliciting internal help to implement a tough plan by using appropriate, persuasive, optimistic language. This style also reveals how Iacocca got more than 450 top managers to leave the relative security of financially sound companies to join a debt-ridden company whose position was derided by the competition, Congress, the press, and the stock market.

He did not accomplish the turnaround by saying, "We'll either turn this company around in a year or two or close it." Yet many managers and business owners use negative, fear-motivated pessimism daily in an effort to implement their plans. Then they deride participants for having low morale.

Iacocca was criticized and denigrated by the press, many lawmakers, and an astute corps of economists, who predicted the demise of Chrysler. His optimism within the Chrysler Corporation, however, was translated as "Together we can do this. With your cooperation we can make this work. We'll build this into a successful, profitable company again with your help."

As the turnaround proceeded, Iacocca was roundly criticized for mentioning Chrysler's positive cash position. The financial press called it braggadocio. One well-known newscaster labeled it an egocentric statement. Nevertheless, consider the impact this statement had on dealers, suppliers, employees—and consumers. It was the same as saying, "With your help we turned this company around, and soon things will be even better."

How does Iacocca rate according to the EPOD theory? He has outstanding high energy. His language was extremely persuasive, very much on target for his dealers, his managers, stockholders, and the general public. Only the press saw his language as ineffective, but he used the press—they were not the constituency he was trying to persuade. His optimism was outstanding. He used strong discipline in timing his forecasts and then following through.

HOW DO YOU FEEL ABOUT YOURSELF?

If you hold a leadership position, how you feel about yourself determines how other people in the environment feel, because you inject either positiveness or negativity into that environment. As an optimistic, visible role model at Wal-Mart, Sam Walton was an impact on two hundred thousand employees (including those hired today). As a leader in a company, association, church, or in your own home, your optimism is crucial.

Our society is beset by a heavy air of negativity by the press. At the close of the 1970s, during the height of unemployment (about 10 percent), the press began circulating stories that stated that "unemployment is now at 10 percent, the highest total since the Great Depression."

Yet who reported that we were still employing 90 percent of our employable work force? Moreover, the comparison with the Great Depression was unfounded. During the Great Depression, 27 percent of the American work force was unemployed. You can't compare 10 percent with what happened in 1930. Do you realize that no other nation with a population of more than 200 million has been able to continually employ 90 percent or more of its available labor?

Pessimism permeates the news media—and we must seek it, or they would not continue to offer it. If the refrigerator were invented today, the "teaser" for the evening news would be "a great calamity has befallen the ice-making industry."

It seems easier to be pessimistic than optimistic in today's society. We have so much, though we value it so little. Most of us live in a world of abundance, yet we cry about what we do not have.

Your customers and your staff are subjected to heavy doses of media negativity. Your deeply felt optimism is a badly needed breath of fresh air on top of being a key ingredient for success.

CUES FROM WITHIN

In a sea of negativeness, it is important to take cues from within and not from those around us. Here is an old story, but it bears repeating:

A farmer operated a successful fruit stand along a country road during the Great Depression. Though, economically, times were bad, this fruit stand enjoyed a healthy business.

With increasing frequency, customers would comment to the farmer that times were tough and perhaps he should cut back. People would say, "Don't you know we're in the middle of a depression?" So he decided to cut back a little on the variety of produce offered. Then he started changing his prices, anticipating what would be effective in this market. As others continued to offer their viewpoint on the economy, he went on making changes.

Within a matter of weeks his business had fallen off considerably, and it never did return to the original level. Times were tough, no question, but to this business the tough time had nothing to do with the Depression—it was self-induced.

DO YOU EVER GET DEPRESSED? I sometimes get asked, "Do you ever get depressed?" My answer is, "Yes and no."

Yes, like all human beings, I get depressed. I have never met a human being who did not get depressed. The no part of my answer is that I do not permit myself to stay depressed. When depression is evident, I don't allow myself the luxury of maintaining it. I won't tolerate it.

Depression doesn't simply come; it comes with your approval. Dr. Wayne Dyer, in *Your Erroneous Zones*, stresses that we can choose our emotions. Much of what we call depression or being down is a choice, not an unantic-ipated, unretractable condition.

THE FALLACY OF BELIEVING THINGS ARE GOING TO GET BETTER

While I maintain an optimistic outlook, I never believe things will get better. This is not contrary to maintaining an optimistic outlook. Rather, this is a stepping stone for action. I don't believe that things will just naturally get better by themselves. It is up to me, and I can take action to make things get better.

If I am selling nine products and the market drys up in three of them, I could lose a third of my volume. However, I am going to invest more energy in the sale of the remaining six products, believing that they are going to make up the difference.

> The resolve to make things better stems not from a whimsical type of optimism based on hopes and wishes, but from an action-orientation that says, "I can make things better."

Optimism is a choice. Pessimism is a choice. Depression is a choice. So, too, happiness is a choice. Abraham Lincoln once said, "Most people are about as happy as they make their minds up to be." More recently, in his book, *Love Is Letting Go of Fear*, Dr. Gerald Jampolsky said, "You can be right or you can be happy"—a very provocative statement.

Does that mean that being right conflicts with being happy?

Often it does. The reason is that, much of the time, other people will not regard you as right (or vice versa), and you'll work so hard to convince them that you will be unhappy in terms of the effort and energy expended in convincing them. Moreover, what is "right"? Your value system versus theirs? Often "right" is simply a difference in value systems.

THE TYPICAL APPROACH TO EACH DAY

Many people approach each new day lying in bed dreading the alarm buzzer. Then it goes off. If they stayed up too late the night before, or had too much to eat, or overexerted themselves, they get up stiff and sore. They drag themselves into the bathroom and groan. According to a Harris Poll, most people are unhappy about the way they look and dress. They do not like the way their hair looks, or they see themselves as too short, too fat, too tall, too thin, too light, or too dark.

Whatever the reason, many people are not happy when starting the day—the most important time of the day to generate optimism. The greatest audience in the world is not your employees, not your customers, and not the people you have to report to.

The greatest audience in the world is the audience of one—you.

If you start with an optimistic view and tell the audience of one what kind of day it will be, your optimism will permeate your relationships and business environment.

"Hold on, Dave. It can't be that simple."

Yes, it can, but it takes practice. Generating optimism is exercise for your mind, just as working out at the health club is exercise for your body.

You can develop bigger biceps by lifting weights; you can increase your level of optimism by lifting your spirits.

START YOUR DAY WITH OPTIMISM

If you would like to experiment, try some of these suggestions and measure whether your "O" factor has increased.

• When you get up in the morning, don't read the front page of the newspaper. Start with the lighter sections such as the sports page or lifestyles, and maybe the comics.
• Turn to the front page last (where you will get a heavy analysis of what's wrong with the world, from an institution steeped in negativity).
• As a daily exercise, when you rise and start to shave or put on your makeup, instead of contemplating what has gone wrong in your life and in your company, and all the things that may go wrong today, choose to acknowledge how far you have come in life—your accomplishments—and how this is going to be a great day.

When I get up in the morning, the first thing I say to myself, out loud, is "This is going to be a great day." Then I say, "This day belongs to me; no one can take it away."

I tell myself I am going to have a great day, because no one else is going to tell me.

My job is to feel good about me. I do not run through a litany of everything that happened the day before—what I liked or didn't like. I do not deal in the long history of what could be seen as negative things that have happened in my life. If some of those thoughts emerge, I view each "negative" event as the positive motivator of where I am headed today.

I bring my optimism to other human beings, especially my staff. Before I get to the office and encounter my employees and my customers, I remember I can carry with me and transmit optimism all day. If I catch my optimism slipping, I repeat my special affirmation:

> I am a unique and precious being created by God for very special purposes. I am ever doing the best I can. I am ever growing in love and awareness.

Then I recite a version for others, because they are unique and precious beings created by God for special purposes, and they are ever doing the best they can. When another person offends you or says something that is inconsistent with your value system, especially remember that they are ever doing the best they can. If they could do better, they would.

Get into action—optimism is ignited by action. If your co-workers or staff are pessimistic, accept the challenge of remaining optimistic. Use centering techniques from BK, or silent affirmations.

When you hear employees say, "This won't work" or "I can't do this" offer them an encouraging, optimistic message, such as "Sure it can, and you're just the person to make it work." Be sure that your employees offer that message to customers.

CASE #45: CREATE LONG-TERM CUSTOMERS

Optimism, like persuasive language, helps develop and maintain long-term customers. Let's return to Alice's service counter. A second customer calls. After gathering the appropriate information, Alice responded with "Bring it in and we'll get to work on it."

A similar response is *not* offered by the competitor company up the street. Customers there are likely to hear "We don't really handle that here," "If you will read Provision #19A of your warranty . . . ," "We can send it down to our plant in New Jersey," or anything that conveys the message "We don't really want to serve you after the sale. We're afraid you are going to squander our time and lower our profitability."

The optimistic company, headed by an optimistic manager, relishes the opportunity to secure another satisfied customer, since having additional contact with customers contributes to the development of long-term relationships. The optimistic manager knows that

> by offering a high degree of service, the probability is raised that others will become dependent upon that service.

He looks forward to opportunities to offer the message "You can depend on us."

OPTIMISM IN ACTION

Perhaps the best example of optimism I have heard was told to me by my Texas-based fellow speaker Senator Bob Murphey. He was waiting for me in the back of the room, dressed in western attire—Stetson hat, string tie, and fancy boots. He said, "Dave, I heard you talkin' 'bout optimism, and I wanna tell you 'bout the most optimistic man I know, my cousin Calvin Lee Rose.

"Calvin Lee," he said, "was running for political office. He went out and picked up the voter registration polls and put 'em over the sun visor of his car—that's how he found people he wanted to talk to.

"He searched out this here woman's house, and he went up and knocked on the door. The woman come to the door, and he swept off his hat and said, 'Good morning, ma'am.

"'My name is Calvin Lee Rose, and I'm arunnin' for assist'nt deputy dog catcher in this town, and I would surely appreciate your vote.' He put his Stetson back on.

"The woman said, 'Calvin Lee Rose, I know you and I knows your whole blessed family, and none of you are any dang good.'

"She said, 'You been divorced three times, you drink whiskey, play cards, and you hung around with loose women most of your life. If you were the only-est man left on the face of the earth, I would not vote for you, and if the buzzards was comin' to look over your body if you dropped dead, I would not shoo 'em. And if you don't get off my porch, I'm agoin' to get my husband's 16-gauge shotgun and fill your posterior with lead.'

"Calvin Lee swept his Stetson off and said to her, 'I thank you, ma'am.'

"He left and got back in his car, removed the voter registration card from the sun visor, searched down until he found that woman's name, held the place with his one thumb, removed the pencil from behind his ear, wet the pencil on his tongue, and wrote after her name 'doubtful.'"

So the question is, how optimistic are you?

HOW OPTIMISTIC AM I?

Points:	[0]	[1]	[2]	[3]
	Never	*Occasionally*	*Frequently*	*Always*

1. Do I start each day with an optimistic self-affirmation such as "This is going to be a great day" or "I am looking forward to today"?
2. Do I understand that most statistics have nothing to do with me, that it is my determination that affects the outcome of situations?
3. Do I project optimism to others?
4. Do I minimize the time spent worrying about competition?
5. Do I avoid losing heart when my ideas are subjected to negativity?

6. Do I regard "objections" as signs of interest?
7. Do I accept compliments about myself graciously and frequently compliment others sincerely?
8. Do I believe that the world is essentially full of good people?
9. Do I believe that if things are going properly, then I can influence them to continue?
10. Do I consciously accept that the mind does not know the difference between the real and the imaginary, and that I can choose to feel happy today?

If you score 15 or less, work on developing an optimistic outlook. Over 20 indicates you are above average yet need more frequency of optimistic feelings. 24 to 28 puts you in an elite group (probably less than 10 percent of the population) with the potential to influence others.

EPOD TACTICS

• The strategy to instill positiveness and optimism starts with the abandonment of old ideas, limits, and problem-solving methods, and with the adopting of new language that eliminates negativity and value judging.

Develop a new language of optimism in your company.

• Often, we are critical of those who are negative. While I have never been criticized for being overly positive, I do find that many people regard this as cockiness. So, be careful in how you extend your positive outlook.

• Try to be totally creative in whatever you attempt to communicate. When I return from a trip, and our furniture has more dust on it than I'd like, instead of being critical, I write "I love you" in the dust.

• If you experience anger towards someone, record your feelings on cassette. When you play the tape back the next day, if you are still angry, add new feelings and subtract what no longer applies. No need to send the tape. This short exercise reduces the energy given to anger and helps you to get on with the business of living.

• Acknowledge that if things are going "too well," it does not mean that something "bad" is going to happen.

• Take full responsibility for your own happiness.

• Avoid phrases such as "Look what you made me do" or "If you hadn't done this, everything would have worked out fine."

• Do not allow yourself to be overly influenced by media statistics, e.g., economic turnarounds, unemployment.

• On the phone—one of two circumstances probably governs the business calls you receive: (1) the caller is already doing business with you and wants to do more, or (2) the caller is interested in buying something from you or is seeking your services for the first time.

Make sure that the phone is used as a tool and not as a weapon. Have the person answering speak slowly and clearly, use an upbeat and enthusiastic voice, and make that caller feel important.

• Accept yourself exactly as you are, with your exact circumstances. This does not mean that you are not going to grow, only that you first accept yourself and love yourself as you are.

• Never devalue or put yourself down. You are a unique creation with the capability to shine. Take care of what God gave you—your body and your mind.

4   Discipline

The major and measurable difference
in the performance of most managers
is how they choose to deal with the
unpleasant or less desirable tasks.
—Dave Yoho

The fourth element of EPOD is discipline, which involves doing all the things you don't like to do and doing most of them well. The lack of discipline is probably the greatest single barrier to getting what we want out of life. If we don't discipline ourselves, then society or nature usually will.

Many people today are prone to the desire for immediate gratification. Young people want the benefits of being adults immediately. New entrants to the labor force want to rise faster than their experience and abilities dictate.

Too often, the inability to delay gratification through self-discipline is the destroyer of people's dreams and goals.

CASE #6: THE DISCIPLINE TO GATHER KNOWLEDGE

C. Ray Johnson, the past president of Coachmen Industries, a major recreational-vehicle manufacturer in the United States, went on to become president of a division of

Kaufman and Broad and ultimately put together a leveraged buy-out before the age of forty.

Effectively managing public corporations, being responsible to accountants, lawyers, the SEC, stockholders, and thousands of employees, setting up plants, buying and selling real estate, and dealing with myriad advertising and public-relation responsibilities might seem impossible for Johnson when you consider that he has only a high school diploma. Yet he may be one of the most educated people I know. What he lacks in formal studies, he makes up for with his discipline.

Johnson, a client and friend, reads every major business book published and maintains a library of business cassettes and videotapes that rivals many retail stores. A disciplined reader and listener, he has cassette players in his car and office and throughout his home, and he maintains a self-designed daily educational program. His follow-through on new ideas is unsurpassed.

Within his busy schedule, he attends several seminars annually, is a member of the Young Presidents Organization, the Sales Executive Club of New York, and many other organizations which gives him an opportunity to network and enhance his knowledge of business.

Johnson's ability to pick apart a financial statement, analyze internal operating conditions, and forecast and accomplish turnarounds is the envy of many business executives. He ranks with the most accomplished people I have cited in publications and speeches, and I always refer to him when I talk about the law of compensating balances. (If you're weak or deficient in one area, you're strong or competent in another.)

CASE #55: USING DISCIPLINE TO KEEP YOUR HEAD WHEN ALL ABOUT YOU ARE LOSING THEIRS

In 1978, when Paul Franks moved to Hilton Head Island, the Sea Pines Real Estate Company was in its heyday. Franks had recently sold his oil distribution business in Atlanta and, after considering other options, decided to sell real estate—something he had never done.

Franks joined a seventeen-person sales organization and rose rapidly. By 1980, he was vice president of residential sales. In 1981, a banner year for the company, he became vice president of real estate, directing fifty salespeople, who produced more than $25 million in sales.

Then a series of reorganizations severely tested Franks's mettle. Over the next six years, Sea Pines was sold, restructured, and reorganized. It fell under the control of seven different management groups, all of whom experienced crippling cash flow, credit, and credibility problems. Through various policy changes, Franks's own office was moved seven times. By mid-1987, a trustee had been appointed to operate the now virtually bankrupt entity.

I had been a consultant of Sea Pines in the early 1980s, and witnessed the degeneration and demotivation of staff relationships. While my contract terminated when the original owners sold out, I continued to follow this organization with great interest. The real estate division, under Franks, continued to expand during this tumultuous period.

Consider the discipline of Paul Franks, who attended executive conferences and was routinely exposed to bad news, reports of insolvency, rapid management changes, and lack of consistency. Despite this, he returned each time to stimulate his sales organization.

Despite the various company problems, Franks's division expanded to more than one hundred salespeople. With sales exceeding $100 million dollars, it became the largest real estate company in South Carolina.

It took great discipline for Franks to stick to his plan, which may seem simple to recite but is a challenge to administer:

- Retain your best salespeople and keep nurturing them.
- Never miss paying a commission check.
- Pay all real estate division bills on time.
- Don't disappoint the purchaser.
- Divorce yourself from the company problems.
- Don't bring bad news back from a meeting.
- Show your salespeople and staff how to effectively deal with poor publicity and rumors.
- Constantly forecast reasonable increases and reach them.

Since 1987, Sea Pines has been owned by residents of the resort community. Thanks to the unwavering success and financial strength of the real estate division, the company has attained solidarity in its financial and administrative structure.

Franks never gave up, and the majority of his staff responded positively to his discipline. To paraphrase Rudyard Kipling: "If you can keep your head when all about you are losing theirs," brother, you've got discipline.

CRUCIAL IN BUSINESS

Discipline or the lack of it plays a major role for a business and for the individuals within that business.

Salespeople seldom like to prepare their call reports, complete paperwork, or make cold calls. Yet these three tasks are basic to the sales role.

Without diligence and discipline, the salesperson will often abandon ongoing efforts and accept the potential of failure. Moreover, sales managers are limited in enforce-ment capabilities. Attempts to force, intimidate, or cajole staffs may work, but for only a brief period. The key is for the salesperson to understand the importance of the less glamorous and exciting tasks, and exhibit a high level of energy in their completion.

Most salespeople would rather call on a familiar face than solicit a new account. Professionals offering services would rather have someone call them than make new sales calls. Salespeople tend to do business with certain types of people and avoid others, regardless of sales potential, and most salespeople would rather make a new sale than service a complaint.

Yet those with discipline recognize the value of servicing complaints, and do it because they realize it will help them reach their goals that much sooner. The same is true for completing paperwork and making cold calls.

Major corporations are highly structured, controlled by stringent policies and plans. Entrepreneurs seldom use any of these controls. In many cases they don't exert the discipline necessary to undertake such plans or the crucial follow-through. Even when they retain an outside consult-ant to prepare a plan, they seldom follow it.

In large corporations, preparing budgets, forecasts, fi-nancial management plans, goals, and quotas is the respon-sibility of assigned managers.

However, these disciplines that are built into corporations are often missing from small businesses. Entrepreneurs who do achieve financial success manage to shorten their work load, heighten their productivity and profitability, and run a more efficient business by exerting more discipline.

FUNDAMENTAL DISCIPLINES

In business, lack of discipline leads to failure. A fundamen-tal discipline is to spend less money than you earn. It may not sound profound, yet it's a difficult discipline for many entrepreneurs, as well as managers in larger organizations, to follow.

There are actually two businesses involved in running a business: the business itself, including its products or services, and the cash flow, which consists of return on investment, return on assets deployed, budgets, forecasting and so on.

Having knowledge of a trade or profession is not the same as running a business. The skilled auto mechanic who wants to open up his own auto repair shop may not be qualified to do so. The talented lawyer in a prestigious law firm who sets off on his own may not have the background necessary to be successful, though his functional capability as a lawyer is excellent.

The business of running a business requires much more than being skilled at the provision of service. It also involves meeting a payroll, being able to make wise purchasing decisions, maintaining a positive cash flow, making hiring and firing decisions, and a host of other responsibilities. Discipline in business often requires going back to basics—rebuilding from the ground up. Many people would rather not.

Learn how to read a balance sheet and income statement. Many people who run their own businesses don't know how and have never taken the time to learn.

Give up tasks. Most entrepreneurs and managers hang on to trivial tasks that they don't need to be handling. Continuous growth in a small business eventually demands that someone else begin opening the mail and ordering supplies rather than the entrepreneur. Likewise, within an organization, if you are a manager or division head, you need to continually assess what you can let go of.

Cast off menial tasks and activities that have been part of your routine and concentrate on other more important things.

Managers who deal in too much trivia cannot be effective interacting with their employees. Even if you are the best at purchasing supplies, assign that task to someone else. That other person may never do the job as effectively as you. However, assigning him or her to handle purchases frees you to close another big deal or to make better long-term plans. Make a list right now of three trivial tasks that you will give up today.

CASE #9: INHERITING THE FAMILY BUSINESS

Peter Heaney, the president of Skaggs-Walsh, a large fuel-oil dealer in metropolitan New York, assumed his post upon the death of his father. At times the pressures of running a business with an established staff, in a highly competitive market, with a constantly changing customer base, and faced with increased volume and decreasing profits seemed more than this 22-year-old could handle.

Heaney, a shy man with an excellent business education from St. Johns University, felt great frustration in attempting to direct a once-viable business now in a fit of decline. Within two years he gained 105 pounds, developed a three-and-a-half-packs-per-day cigarette habit, and began downing a couple martinis a day to ease the pressures.

When Heaney became our client, I took into consideration all the aforementioned conditions and suggested the following: that he develop a new training discipline for his salespeople, change his marketing thrust, and restructure his organization. I also requested that he participate on service calls, including inquiries for new oil customers and those seeking estimates for new equipment.

Any one of these changes would have been a considerable task for the average individual. The latter suggestion was antithetical to this young man's behavioral structure. However, with the support of his wife Joan and a prewritten marketing plan, he set out to both restructure the company and learn the basics.

The initial resistance from his own salespeople, coupled with his lack of understanding of the sales role, presented extreme challenges. Yet within less than a year the following had happened: Peter had installed a training regimen for his salespeople for which he had become the pilot. For three out of the next twelve months he was the top producer in his sales organization. He wrote a new computer program and developed the software to implement the marketing plan, gaining a reputation in his market territory as a leader in sales and service. His prices were not the lowest, yet dozens of customers wrote about the efficiency and effectiveness of his company.

Without discipline he would have given up after one month. It took much longer than that to get the whole process working, but Heaney stayed on course. Subsequently, he sent me this letter (1978):

We attempted to follow the guidelines which you recommended as closely as possible and, frankly, this became our greatest profit year. As you will see in the attached chart, we actually doubled the number of accounts.

As an added benefit, our bank (Chemical) was equally impressed. Last year our line of credit was $1,350,000, and this year we have reduced our borrowing to $750,000.

In addition, we now have on deposit over $400,000 in either CD's or T-Bills, and in the same period last year the balance on our loan was $550,000.

I am almost afraid to ask—what do we do now?

Peter F. Heaney
President
Skaggs-Walsh, Inc.
College Point, NY

Today Peter, forty-nine, is a shining example of discipline. He is a svelte one hundred pounds lighter, nonsmoking, nondrinking business executive who plays tennis twice weekly. He's acquired two additional companies equal in size to his first and is negotiating to buy one more. In January of 1989 he received an honorary doctorate from St. John's University.

Disciplined individuals master the art of engaging in that which they prefer not to do.

DISCIPLINE: INTERNAL OR EXTERNAL

Discipline means preparing for and adjusting to changes in your marketplace, the economy, and public taste. Discipline means not permitting others to convince you that things are rotten. It means avoiding those people or situations that create doubt or lower your integrity or morals.

The discipline that you display has a strong impact on your associates and customers. Everything you do in life and in business is based either on discipline or a lack of it.

If you do not discipline yourself, society, nature, or customers will.

If you overeat, your cardiovascular system will make you pay. If you smoke, your lungs will respond. If you don't exercise discipline in your business, you may fail. If you spend more than you take in, you will be disciplined: by banks, creditors, suppliers, the IRS, and your inability to meet payroll.

CASE # 1: DISCIPLINE YOURSELF OR BE DISCIPLINED

Prior to speaking at a conference one morning, I tested the sound system after returning from a jog. A woman came by and noticed that I was in my sweat suit, headband, and running shoes. She inquired, "Oh, you're a runner?" I responded, "Thirty years." She said, "You must love it."

"No," I said, "it is drudgery. I have been rained on, hosed down, and bitten by dogs. I have had twisted ankles, and endured aches, pains, and muscle pulls."

"Then why do you do it?" she asked.

"Because the discipline of jogging five days a week keeps my cardiovascular system in top shape." My pulse rate is 52 standing and 44 resting. This is one of the major factors that enabled me to complete 137 speeches last year, plus 12 training video programs and numerous radio and television appearances, while still running a consulting group.

CASE #3: DISCIPLINE TO LOSE WEIGHT

Let's say you are forty-seven pounds overweight and would you like to lose that weight. Don't go on a diet, because starting a diet is not an effective application of the EPOD Theory. Instead draw upon your discipline capabilities and cut out one thing at a time.

Harold Waller removed butter from his diet for twenty-one days and lost some weight. Then he began another 21-day cycle and removed bread from his diet. Then he took out meat. In the fifth 21-day period, he limited his alcohol consumption to two glasses per week. After 105 days, he had lost a total of 35 pounds and began a new regimen to maintain his new, lower weight.

You can lose weight, and you don't have to go on some kind of earth-shattering diet. If you are clinically obese and have been under a doctor's care, this doesn't apply to you.

If you have average health and happen to be overweight, cut just one item from your diet for a 21-day period. For a start, try butter. You will lose weight.

CASE #57: NOT YOUR AVERAGE STANDOUT ATHLETE

> If you want to excel in almost anything, devote at least 10,000 hours to practice it.
>
> —Bob Richards

Are you old enough to remember Bob Richards, the man who graced the Wheaties cereal box and was their spokesman for thirteen years? He came to prominence as a 21-year-old pole-vaulter in the 1948 Olympics. He won the Bronze Medal that year, and in 1952 and 1956 won the Gold Medal.

At five-foot-ten in height and 175 pounds, Bob Richards didn't seem the most likely candidate to bring home the gold. However, Richards had a strong belief in himself, and dedicated more than ten thousand hours to training. In 1951, 1954, and 1955 he entered the national competition in the decathlon. He didn't win, but he had a masterful showing against Goliaths such as Milt Campbell, at six-four, 225 pounds, and Rafer Johnson, at six-four and 210 pounds.

Today Bob Richards, at sixty-six, hasn't lost his fire. Bob and I often share the same platform. Once I introduced him to some young friends of mine who had come to hear me speak. At the conclusion of his presentation he did a handstand, and from that position did ten push-ups! Bob competes in the "Master" Olympics and is still setting world records in the pole-vault.

REACHABLE AND REWARDING

Discipline is acquired; it is not something that you are born with. Ask yourself what the greatest skill is that you bring to your work or profession. Is it stamina, endurance, leadership, believability, interpersonal skills, loyalty, dedication? Whatever it is, I guarantee you were not born with it; you acquired it as a result of life experiences that taught you the value or need of developing what you developed.

So, too, the successful entrepreneur and the successful business adopt those disciplines that enable them to survive and prosper in the long run.

Discipline is the make or break component of the EPOD Theory.

In alliance with energy, persuasiveness, and optimism, the business and the individual possessing discipline have all the tools of success. In the absence of discipline, all the energy, persuasiveness, and optimism in the world may not be enough.

HOW DISCIPLINED AM I?

Points:	[0]	[1]	[2]	[3]
	Never	*Occasionally*	*Frequently*	*Always*

1. Do I create a plan for my new business direction or lifestyle change?
2. Do I consciously work on changing habits that are not in my best interest?
3. Have I been successful in ridding myself of habits that are not in my best interest, e.g., overeating, smoking, drinking?

4. Do I use part of each day to learn something new?
5. If I am required to perform an undesirable task, do I bring high energy to the task?
6. Do I research the breakdowns in my interaction with others to determine a source and corrective process?
7. Do I maintain a positive attitude during periods of change?
8. Do I set long-range goals, break them down into groups and track them on a regular basis?
9. When I am partially successful in goal completion do I maintain commitment to the project?
10. Do I work well with others who have habits or behave in a way of which I do not approve?

10 to 15 indicates a low level of discipline; 16 to 20, a moderate level; 21 to 24, an effective level; and 25 or higher, excellent.

EPOD TACTICS

• Nature helps, but it's nurture that counts most. Society continues to debate what makes one individual successful while another fails: nature or nurture? I've seen enough cases to believe it's nurture. If average individuals exert the proper discipline, they will become successful.

• Plan the next day's activities before leaving the office. The simple discipline of scratching a note to yourself indicating the three or four priorities of the next work day alerts you to what you can look forward to.

• To ward off "unmanageable stress" in the work place requires discipline. Don't take on a heavier work load than is reasonable. Don't make impractical time commitments and deadlines. Don't overreact to people who have incompatible behavior styles to yours. Get sufficient and regular feedback.

• Make memos to yourself on everything you have done and will do, and what you are thinking.

• Acquire the habit of thoroughly reading anything that is boring but beneficial.

• Take an extra five minutes to communicate with someone who you do not easily understand.

• Devote twenty-one days to effect a behavioral change in some area of interest to you.

• Discipline in starting a business today: Design the environment to accommodate the customer rather than the employee.

• IN ESTABLISHED COMPANIES: If you run a business that was established years ago, examine your environment, see if it accommodates the customer, and redesign accordingly.

Create a methodology for each task, from answering the phone to responding to the most complex problem. The methods will be part of what we call "the system". Everyone should be taught the system and encouraged to practice it and pass it on. Each office should have a sign which says, "The System Reigns Supreme."

The following is a partial "conversion" list that we frequently give to clients with established businesses. Some of the items in this list apply to small businesses as well as to those who simply need redirection. The key element is whether the general manager or CEO will exercise the discipline necessary to see that these ideas are fulfilled.

1. Stop opening the mail.
2. Don't make the bank deposit yourself. If you structure financing for your customers, don't take the "deals" to the bank.
3. Develop a weekly cash report system. Indicate daily or weekly deposits, sources, total cash, items in transit or limbo, cash needs for the week.
4. Tell employees what you want done, instead of telling them what to do each day.

5. Don't buy stock, inventory, or advertising on impulse. Use a plan (budget/forecast) method and review it on a programmed basis.
6. Delegate whenever possible.
7. Send a letter to all your vendors, large and small, requesting prompt-payment discounts. First state your satisfaction with their product or service, then indicate your interest in saving by improving your business relations.
8. If you are paying your staff on a weekly basis, change it to a biweekly basis. You will write twenty-six less checks per person per year, improve your cash flow, and reduce the accounting entries.

MANAGING THE BUSINESS ELEMENTS

In the next four chapters we'll take a look at how the EPOD elements can be applied to the tough challenges you face in managing your business or your career. Chapter 5, "The Power Plan," discusses why putting your thoughts and plans on paper is so important, particularly when it comes to financial matters.

Chapter 6, "Changing the Rules," reveals why you are in control of the situations in your life and how to creatively approach them to gain strategic advantage. It offers numerous examples of individuals who took control of an environment, applied the elements of the EPOD Theory, and turned the tide of events to their favor.

Chapter 7, "Selling," shatters many of the prevailing myths about selling and replaces them with more effective methods and guidelines to help master this crucial component of business. It also introduces co-communication, a powerful tool with which to interact with others.

Chapter 8, "Negotiating Agreements and Retaining Outside Help," provides a framework by which you can learn to structure your own effective agreements. It also offers guidelines on selecting and retaining professional help such as lawyers, accountants, and consultants.

5   The Power Plan

To know and not to do
is not to know.
                                                    —Zen

Fifteen hundred and sixty weeks equal a career.
When I ask audiences what they will do with the next 1,560
weeks, after the puzzled looks and head scratching, someone usually figures out that 1,560 weeks equals 30 years,
about the length of a career.

The student about to enter college is saddled with a heavy
responsibility—what courses to choose. The choices may
affect how he or she makes a living and his or her happiness
for decades to come. Yet the student has only lived 25
percent of his or her expected life, most of it as a child.

Students and young professionals frequently stumble
along on decisions made with limited input or knowledge.
There are many who choose to be lawyers because of
parental influence or because they have seen sixteen epi-
sodes of "L.A. Law."

While the path that leads people to their initial occupations may be jagged, what's worse is that they usually
continue even further without a plan.

BEFORE ALL, A PLAN

When people read books such as this one, often what they
are really seeking is a magical formula that is going to make
them successful. I have clients who say, Come in and make

us rich. The first thing we do, however, is formulate a business plan.

The person who is forty pounds overweight wants to know how to lose it instantly. However, you accumulate weight the same way you accumulate behavior, a little bit at a time. You can only take off weight a layer at a time. Likewise, you can only take off behavior a layer at a time.

Usually people change for three basic reasons: (1.) They've become bored. (2.) There is much pain connected to what they are doing. (3.) They've come to realize they can change. If you want to change your behavior, work on one or two aspects of it at a time, not nine or ten.

EVERYONE NEEDS A POWER PLAN

You need a power plan to help you move from where you are to where you want to be. A power plan can reflect what you are capable of doing, how you will interact with others, and how you feel about yourself. An effective power plan involves scrapping a lot of old formulas and substituting new ones, and it requires energy and personal discipline.

I suggest you produce a personal power plan for the next 360 days and, for each particular goal or quest, a mini power plan, requiring no more than one page, to keep you on track.

Suppose you are going to jog. On January 1 you decide how many miles per day, where, and how frequently you are going to jog. How many miles will you complete in a year? If you travel, what kind of clothes will you pack? If you don't produce a written plan, halfway through the year you are going to find reasons not to jog. If the weather is good, you will; if it is not, you won't. Eventually you may say, "I used to jog but I gave it up because . . ."

Even if you win the lottery tomorrow, you'll need a plan to handle the two hundred thousand dollars a year you'll collect. Will you still go to work? In what kind of house are you going to live? On what kind of budget will you live? When a widow inherits her husband's estate, frequently and regardless of the size of the estate, the assets are dissipated within seven to ten years. Many lottery winners who receive lump sum payoffs don't fare much better.

Root yourself in reality. Most people who talk about achieving success don't spend much time actually planning for it—rearranging goals, priorities, and activities based on how their life is going to be. Entrepreneurs in particular are notorious nonplanners.

People who fantasize about having their own business focus on the flexibility, being their own boss, and the amount of dollars that will roll in. Few envision the tremendous number of hours that will be required to deal with other people: creditors, suppliers, employees, business partners, and customers.

When the reality of the efforts required to accomplish goals sets in, many people drop back to where they were, and thus little progress toward goals ever occurs.

Unless you have a power plan that enables you to structure your efforts, any decision you make will be made in the context of old behavior and habitual patterns. A written plan aids you in changing behavior and staying focused.

PLANNING ALWAYS HELPS

If you are an outgoing, aggressive type of person who wants to excel in customer service, you need a plan outlining ways you can let the customer be "right," instead of yourself.

If you operate a business and sell one product now but

wish to offer two new products, your transition will be much smoother if you devise a plan, however brief, that pinpoints how you intend to introduce the new products. The plan need not be more than one printed page. It can be in "pros and cons" or in outline form. It should logically carry you through the steps that you anticipate will be necessary to successfully market two more products, but it should not be etched in stone. As you implement initial steps, other parts of the plan may require modification.

FROM PLANS TO SIMPLE SYSTEMS

When I construct a plan that represents a way of doing something that will be repeated, I often divide the plan into modules. For example, I developed a system of training called "Six Steps to a Sale." I took every step in the sales cycle, from the primary contact to the conclusion, and broke it into steps, each having substeps.

I then trained and coached my staff this way, and it became the method by which our sales system functioned. When a phone inquiry came in, the plan spelled out how it was to be handled, e.g., what would be said, the kind of form on which the inquiry would be recorded, and so forth.

I spend the time to plan and organize, because without these tools my business wouldn't grow.

If you were to take an automobile trip of one thousand miles and you had never been to the destination before, you would take a road map. Yet people routinely get up each morning with no map—no plan—and expect to arrive somewhere.

PLANNING FOR GROWTH

You recently started a small business. I ask you if the business is structured to do a million dollars, and you answer, "We are only planning to do a hundred thousand the first year." But if within five years you progress to sales of $1 million, how will you manage the company? Will you have a numbering sequence for your products or services to maintain control? Will you have a billing procedure? A method for handling cash?

As you approach realization of goals, it is not a time to let down your guard.

Too many entrepreneurs who get on a growth cycle can't deal with the success when it comes, because they haven't planned for it.

Don't be worried that your plan may be too premature. No plan is too premature. Any plan is better than no plan. All plans are subject to change.

The value of the planning process comes in the exercise of planning itself, not necessarily the validity of the plan, because you cannot know when you have the "perfect" plan anyway.

Checkbook management is not planning. Suppose you are a small business owner, and you have made a decision to get involved in direct mail. You spend fifteen thousand dollars on a direct mail campaign, and it goes bust. If the money for that campaign was part of operating capital, then you have put your business in jeopardy. But if it was financed with reserves held for this type of venture, you are still in relatively good shape.

Plan-oriented businesses build up such funds. Those without plans operate via checkbook management. This method is typified by the company or individual who sees a fair amount of money in the checkbook and then decides to make a purchase. This is a reckless way of managing finances.

On a personal basis, the checkbook manager is stung every time his car needs a major repair or a home appliance gives out unexpectedly.

The checkbook manager frequently finds himself undertaking deficit spending and financial management using credit cards, so he is always paying the most for needed goods and services. He is dealing from a position of weakness.

When you have assets, you can buy things for less money. Suppliers are more inclined to do business with and offer more favorable terms to a firm or individual who pays promptly. Banks are willing to give lower interest rates to customers with lots of assets. The person with a plan who acquires assets usually pays less and gets more.

Part of an effective power plan is to have cash in the company. You take advantage of prompt payment discounts, buy in sufficient quantities to ensure the best price, and purchase off-season or during a supplier's downtime.

A company or individual is wise to accumulate cash, as well as other liquid assets, for many reasons. In an accelerating economy, replacement costs are usually higher than original costs. A piece of equipment purchased for $100,000, with depreciation will have a book value of a few thousand dollars. When it is time to replace that equipment, it may cost $150,000 versus $100,000 originally.

If you accumulate an additional ten thousand dollars for each of five years, when it comes time to buy the new equipment, you might have the capital to do so; you'd at least have assets to borrow against to acquire the equipment. The key is to have the equipment generate revenues in excess of its depreciation each year.

FINANCIAL POWER PLANNING

In producing your financial power plan, your credit rating is one of your most valuable assets. Look for ways to keep it strong. It will pay off over and over again. If you have a strong credit rating, you can get almost anything you want. People who don't know you want to give you goods, offer you loans, and make deals with you.

When someone wants to check out our credit rating or look at our financial statements, we are pleased to have them do so. When we negotiate with a supplier, we are in an advantageous position. From the outset we have frequently received terms that suppliers reserve for their best and longest-standing customers. Often they give us a better price than one we'd ask them for.

Even as an individual, you can produce your own financial power plan by looking for ways to build up your bank accounts, developing a track record of paying your bills promptly, and positioning yourself for large purchases using financial or credit information as leverage. Let's look at some key strategies.

Borrow money when you don't need it, to establish credit—In my twenties I took out a hundred thousand dollar loan that I really did not need and could repay immediately. The reason? By taking out this loan, and quickly repaying, I established a track record. When I needed funds of more than a hundred thousand dollars and I went back to the bank, they looked up my records and then offered me another loan. I established a springboard from which I could quickly acquire a loan when I needed one. I used this method and was able to borrow $1 million before I was thirty years old.

Start that IRA, if you qualify; if you don't, start one for your children—Many people fail to get an IRA, believing that two thousand dollars is required before starting one. You can put as little into an IRA as you choose and add to it at your own pace. Remember you earn nontaxable interest.

Invest in savings bonds—When a client or friend has a new baby, I suggest they start a U.S. savings bond program in the name of their child. Bonds are purchased at 50 percent of face value and mature in seven years. Taxes on the modest interest they earn do not have to be paid until maturity. Since it's the child's interest, it can be delayed and will usually be at a very low rate.

Bonds represent an easy, yet solid, investment plan. I recommend that even my childless clients invest a modest amount in a U.S. savings bond plan each year.

PLANNING FOR WHEN THE MONEY COMES

If you are twenty-eight years old and are making thirty thousand dollars a year, how are you going to spend your money when you're making fifty-two thousand? What are you going to invest in? Begin now to devise a plan for how you are going to manage that greater income.

"But, Dave, I've never earned that much, so what is the point of trying? Can't I make a plan as I approach it?"

Begin formulating the plan right now, and you'll see what the point is: your personal horizons will open up. You begin to consider options that were not in your consciousness before. Should I invest in real estate, in bonds, or start a retirement plan?

You find yourself reading about these potential investments. As you receive more raises, you become knowledgeable about preserving your capital. You are more inclined to put the money into investment vehicles that can further accelerate progress toward long-term goals.

Do you plan to get married and have children in a few years? That takes money. Would you like to be earning a passive income—interest, dividends, real estate rentals, and so on? Do you want to be able to retire at fifty or sixty? Write down the plan now. Estimate the cost of your future plan in terms of income, using the increase in the last twenty years' cost-of-living index as a projection. Structure an investment plan now and project its growth.

RULE OF 72

To figure out how long it will take your money to double, divide 72 by the rate of interest on your savings:

72 divided by 10 percent = 7.2 years
72 divided by 8 percent = 9.0 years
72 divided by 5 percent = 14.4 years

A PART OF THE PLAN SHOULD BE "BEFRIEND THY BANKER." If you seek a home mortgage, the best bank to do business with is the one where you keep your savings account. When I negotiate a mortgage and have a healthy savings account with the bank, I refuse to pay points.

First I ask for a mortgage commitment. Then I request that the loan officer evaluate what I have in his bank—my accounts, which earn the bank enough of a return so that they do not require that I pay points on mortgage loans. If you run your own business, this tactic will work well for you. Put your excess cash in a short-term certificate of deposit with the bank from which you will be seeking a mortgage. You'll need discipline not to touch the money.

"I am only twenty-five years old, I don't run my own business, and I have no experience with bankers. What do I do?"

Go to an established bank, pick out a loan officer who looks like someone with whom you can communicate, introduce yourself, and say, "I am here to establish a relationship with you. I want to put my savings here, start a checking account, establish trust funds for my children (once I have them), establish a retirement account, and I want to acquire mortgages."

Most bankers will be responsive to this kind of presentation from a well-dressed twenty-five-year-old. Later, when you seek to acquire a mortgage commitment, go back to the banker and say, "I have these assets invested in the bank, what will you do for me?" If he or she can't think of anything, offer suggestions.

All the while you keep building a relationship so that the bank maintains an interest in you and your accounts and is responsive to your needs. If the bank is not responsive, go to another bank.

I have always done business with a major bank at one of their nearby branches. I seek out the manager of the branch with whom I am to have my special banking relationship. I send deposits to him. The bank can't be an amorphous entity to me, and I can't be an insignificant entity to them. I strive to develop a solid interpersonal relationship.

When I need help, I call the manager. I tell him my goals and aspirations. I used the EPOD elements in all aspects of my communication with him. If a competitive banker's CD rates go up $\frac{1}{4}$ percent, I don't jump to the next bank. I remain loyal, knowing that a few points here and there in the long run are not as important as the relationship I am building. I let the banker know this.

MAKE YOUR MONEY WORK FOR YOU. Seek to have several sources of income. It does not make any difference how minor your salary is: you can put your money to work for you. Most people's primary source of income is their paycheck or, if self-employed, the amount they can draw from their business.

Secondary sources of income may be derived from home-based businesses including hobbies that generate income, an investment program, or simple interest from a savings account in the bank. Start from wherever you are; make it a part of your plan. Work toward having income from different sources so you won't be at the mercy of any particular source.

"But, Dave, I have three kids and the bills just keep coming."

CASE # 3: NO MATTER HOW LITTLE YOU EARN

My maternal grandfather, Aaron Jacoby, was illiterate, yet had a greater impact on me than any other man. My grandmother had diabetes, developed glaucoma, and went blind, and they had no hospitalization insurance. Though he only made forty dollars a week, he bought his house and every other possession with cash. He paid my grandmother's hospital bills, and when he died he left an estate of fourteen thousand dollars. If my estate equals $100 million when I die, I will not have accomplished what that man did.

I learned from him that if you have a dollar, you spend eighty cents. If you have ten dollars you spend nine dollars. It doesn't matter what you have, put a piece of it away.

Somehow, some way, you can find room for savings. Economize. Delay the frequency of trading in your car. Don't keep too much money in a demand account that does not pay interest.

Never pay interest on credit cards. I use a credit card for convenience and to temporarily delay payments. Once the bill comes, however, I pay the balance in full. I refuse to pay what amounts to exorbitant interest (14 to 20 percent on some cards). Unfortunately most people use their credit cards inappropriately and end up paying dearly for the privilege. My personal power plan includes not paying more than I have to.

In business my power plan is to always pay and take advantage of the early payment discount that suppliers offer. Even if I had a cash flow problem, I would go out and borrow the money in order to take advantage of suppliers' discounts. Why? The money I would save by making early payments to suppliers would more than offset the cost of the borrowed funds.

2 percent prompt-payment discounts taken regularly earn 37 percent when compounded annually.

PLANNING FOR THE FUTURE, WHICH SNEAKS UP FAST

Less than 0.5 percent of all the mortgages issued in the United States are ever prepaid. If you have a $150,000, thirty-year mortgage at 10 percent, you will be paying $473,889.60 during the life of the loan. Reduce the total amount of your home mortgage by nearly 24 percent by making thirteen payments each year.

With thirteen payments per year, instead of twelve, total interest over the life of the loan decreases $113,000, and the mortgage is fully paid nine years earlier.

Alternatively, instead of getting a thirty-year mortgage, get a twenty-year or a fifteen-year mortgage. You pay only slightly more each month, but you also accelerate the process radically of repaying your loan and reducing your interest costs.

$150,000 mortgage at 10% for 30 years = $1316.36/month payment
$150,00 mortgage at 10% for 15 years = $1611.91/month payment

Payment difference per month = $295.55
Savings over term of mortgage = $183,146.00

With even mild price appreciation, you will develop a large equity in your home that will help you at a time in your life when you need it the most, for example when your kids are about to go to college.

To comfortably send your children to college, if you are making $35,000 a year now, save $4,000 per year. As your income (and resulting savings) increase, in ten or fifteen years you can have $75,000, $100,000, or more invested. From that you educate your children or get extra enjoyment out of life, and you don't have to go into debt.

> You need plans that balance the long term with the short term, because we all have an inherent bias for focusing on the short term

"Don't tell me about fifteen years from now, I've got trouble making ends meet today."

To have a great year every year, continually look past the initial challenge of a new home purchase, starting a business, or changing a career to the reality of what it will take to make the decision succeed.

PLANNING YOUR PSYCHIC INCOME

Psychic income refers to that which is beyond monetary income, such as the enjoyment you derive from running your business or advancing your career. The friendships and associations you make are also contributors to psychic income. Network with those from whom you can learn and with whom you are willing to share.

> Particularly seek affiliations a level or two above your own current knowledge, through clubs, associations, or other groups that offer a broad range of contacts and which introduce a wide range of ideas.

For nearly thirty years I have been a member of the Sales Executive Club (SECNY) of New York, which provides a forum and rich source of "power plan" information. Each week, they sponsor luncheons with speakers ranging from the President of the United States to every visible business leader. I have heard Henry Kissinger, Bill Marriott, and David Ogilvy among many others.

Annually for the past fifty years, to a packed house at the Waldorf Astoria Grand Ballroom, guest speaker Leo Cherne, Chairman of the Research Institute of America, has provided SECNY members with his predictions on the world scene.

"I recommend the club to all my clients. Contact:

> Sales Executive Club of New York
> 114 East 32nd Street, #1301
> New York, NY 10016

DISCIPLINE AND PLANNING

What does it take to execute these types of strategies? A power plan and discipline. The way you devise the plan itself, however, aids in generating discipline. The plan is a discipline.

Some of what you have earned in the early years can be squirreled away for the later years. This viewpoint is nothing new, but the necessity of having a plan to do this is more important than ever. If you are borrowing up to the hilt, your power plan should begin with how you are going to get yourself out of debt. From there your plan details what you will save each month and how much you are going to accumulate by 199x or 20xx.

EPOD TACTICS

• Take advantage of prompt-payment discounts when you are able to do so. Otherwise, pay your bills over the longest period of time and collect the money owed you as promptly as possible. This doesn't mean you cheat your suppliers—negotiate with them for favorable terms.

• Collections are an important part of any business. They help to improve your cash flow and reduce the need to borrow.

• Just before charging a purchase on your credit card, ask the vendor for a discount if you pay cash immediately. Seek a discount equal to what the vendor pays the credit card company.

• Eliminate products or services that don't pull their weight. If an item represents only 5 to 7 percent of your annual volume, unless there is a strong customer service reason to keep it, get rid of it and concentrate on your other products.

• All entrepreneurs experience their share of disappointing developments. You believe you're on the right track, and suddenly a shortage in a critical material cripples your business and cash flow. These phenomena, however, are usually temporary; you can always work around them.

6 Changing the Rules

Lord make me an instrument . . .
Where there is despair, let me sow hope.
—St. Francis of Assisi

What do Robert Redford, Tom Cruise, Paul Newman, Sylvester Stallone, and Dustin Hoffman all have in common? They are all short, standing less than five-ten, and though we tend to value the tall athletic look, these Hollywood screen actors are among the silver screen's great romantic leads.

What was the driving, underlying force in the lives of these actors to become larger-than-life characters on the screen? I believe they had a deep-seated need to achieve and to compensate for their shortness of stature. Consciously or unconsciously, it is likely each actor sought what he needed to do to counteract this situation.

CASE #298: THE SHORT SHALL INHERIT THE SLAM DUNK TITLE

Spud Webb, the explosive guard for the Atlanta Hawks of the National Basketball Association, is listed at five feet, eight inches, but his real height is closer to five-six. He plays in a game where tall men reign supreme, yet he won the NBA slam dunk contest in 1986 over a field of superstars eight to fourteen inches taller than he is. The basket is ten feet high, but to slam dunk you must be able to reach well over the basket. To dunk, Webb jumps nearly his own height.

The conventional wisdom in basketball is that a five-foot-six player simply cannot compete, let alone be a slam dunk champion. Nevertheless, Webb changed the rules for himself and others, such as five-foot-three Tyrone Bogues, who made the NBA in 1988. Webb compensates for his height by working out, doing various leg muscle–building exercises. He doesn't play by convention; he uses his blazing speed to drive past taller opponents.

Because he is shorter, and closer to the floor, his ball handling is surer. When he hunches over while driving to the basket or passing to a teammate, he forces taller opposing guards to look down at an uncomfortable angle. Spud Webb, like many achievers, has learned to change the rules.

CASE #2: WINNING OUR INDEPENDENCE

Some two hundred years ago the rules of warfare were vastly different from today. Opposing armies identified themselves with distinctive uniforms. They fought in open fields. On holidays or during inclement weather they abstained from combat.

How did the American colonists win the Revolutionary War from the British? Behind trees, on Sundays, and in the rain.

CHANGING THE RULES IN BUSINESS

Show me your competition. Are they all large companies? Examine what they are doing.

Accomplish the same results as your competitors in a different way or even in the exact opposite manner.

CASE #154: NOT JUST ANOTHER SOAP COMPANY

When I was in college, we studied business case histories. The soap industry made profits in pennies and competitors often ate each other. Of dozens of industries that start small, you wouldn't choose to go into the soap business. But one company that started small and bucked the trends is now internationally known.

That company was Amway. Their first product? A biodegradable soap, which they sold by changing the rules. They sold their soap via multilevel marketing (on a direct basis), while Proctor and Gamble continued to sell their product through the supermarkets and convenience stores.

Amway sold its product through direct salespeople. Their products had distinctive labeling and packaging as well as an advertising "story," which could be told person to person. All of which represented a major change from the traditional methods of selling soap products. What started as a simple (yet different) kind of soap company now has an estimated volume of $1 billion in annual revenue.

Another innovator is Domino's Pizza, which became successful by changing the rules. To the average palate, pizza is pizza. Domino's guaranteed delivery in under thirty minutes, or the buyer would get three dollars off.

How did Pepsi-Cola, a distant number two in bottled beverages, outsell Coca-Cola in the food market chains? Pepsi invested heavily in the blow-and-fill plastic bottle, which represented a major rule change. The larger, see-through, easily disposable containers could be produced much more cost effectively than smaller bottles. Pepsi was able to sell its product at an attractive price in containers that held more and displayed the contents to the consumer. By changing the rules, they dominated the supermarket shelf.

McDonald's devised a fast-food delivery system that could be administered by young people working at minimum wage. By doing this they drastically lowered labor costs and increased the probability that each outlet would be profitable.

You can change the rules. Regardless of the situation, you have control over your immediate environment. You can change the subject in a classroom. When I had professors that were dull and I couldn't make it through the day, I would change the subject. I would say, "Professor, I have always been curious about ABC. How does this relate to the issue?"

When the professor expanded on that subject, I got through that day in class. By challenging the professor, I changed the plan and learned, rather than staying bored and gaining nothing. In a similar manner you can change the rules in business, regardless of your position or situation.

CASE #138: MAKING THE SUPERMARKET A FRIENDLIER PLACE

Bob O'Brien, twenty, works in a supermarket. He doesn't have a college education, and the thought of using a computer scares him. Still, Bob wants to rise to the management level. So he makes himself indispensable.

Bob goes to the assistant manager and says, "I've been filling the stock shelves. I know the guy out packing the stock is overloaded with work. I'd like to help him and learn how the stock comes in." After a few days Bob knows two jobs. Next, Bob volunteers to help in purchasing.

Soon, in a supermarket with twenty-eight different jobs, Bob knows twenty of them through practical experiences.

Who will be fired last? Bob, because he can fill in at twenty positions. Bob has actually changed the rules.

I WAS A CHRONIC RULE CHANGER

Upon reflection, I realize that I got through my life by continually changing the rules, each time I faced a challenge. While in grade school, I was overweight and often picked on by the other children. Many days I didn't even want to go to school.

In my early teens I began working out and became leaner. The years of being picked on hardened me and convinced me of the importance of self-defense. By fifteen, I had become a street fighter and, amazingly, an amateur boxer.

You were probably not a street fighter or an amateur boxer, but you do have anger and frustrations that are in many ways analogous to being a fighter. In time, I transferred the philosophy of fighting and applied it to much of what goes on in selling.

CASE #12: WHO'S IN CHARGE?

When I was the sales manager of Shield Chemical, I sought an appointment with a man who was very difficult to get to see. I finally got an appointment and, on the day, showed up for it on time at 9:00 A.M. At 9:30, the man came out of his office and joked with the secretaries but still hadn't acknowledged my presence.

At 10:00 I said to the receptionist, "When is he going to see me?" She said, "I don't know, he is very busy." I said, "How busy can he be, he was just out here?" She said, "He will see you when he can see you."

I was about to throw my card down and tell *them* to get in touch with *me*, a useless gesture. I was irritated, and my anger and hostility were about to show themselves until I reflected on something I learned as a boxer: Don't get angry. If the other guy gets angry, he'll make a mistake. If you stay cool, you always have the advantage.

When you allow anger to dominate, you thwart your skills and let the opposition dictate your game plan.

As I looked around the sales manager's reception area, I realized he was frustrating me. I was allowing my anger to make me weak and incautious. When you are angry or feel hostile, you do not function or sell well.

This was a sizable account and I wanted it; I decided to sit patiently for him, however long it took. I picked up a magazine and waited. Ultimately he would come to me. And when he did, guess who was in charge? I was.

Now, you don't respond to someone else's tactics on all occasions—you measure whether the game is worth the prize. In this case it was also a learning experience that has come in handy hundreds of times.

EVERYONE CAN CHANGE THE RULES

Whatever impediments and obstacles you had early in life, it's likely that they are still present in some form. Each of us has the capability to reflect on our life's experiences, learn from them, and apply them in positive ways.

For many years I was in speech therapy and I hated it. People laughed at me. I felt that I was the lowest form of human being. I was forced to speak in front of groups. Sometimes, the harder I tried, the more hopeless the situation seemed. After years of training, however, I was able to speak proficiently and now make my living by speaking.

I now realize that I received an unusual degree of early training on a topic that the typical adult would prefer to avoid: speaking to others, particularly public speaking. The impediment and the lessons I hated slowly became my forte. My weakness became my strength.

Here's a litany of "impediments" that one may face and how to change the rules about them.

125 pounds overweight	Open a big man or woman's store. Work with other obese people on a clinical basis.
Chronically underfinanced, always in debt	Seek partners and joint ventures and, most importantly, get someone else to manage your finances. Meanwhile, capitalize on what you do well.
Inferiority complex	Get involved with counseling and therapy that leads *you* to work with others who are struggling with similar or worse problems. You will gain confidence and improve your relations with others.
High school dropout and teenage mother	Work in a long-term health care facility for the elderly, where you will be surrounded by people who could use a surrogate grandchild.

Poor writing skills	Find other ways to give written reports, hire a ghost writer, take a course, buy software that checks spelling and grammar, record your work on a cassette. Also, manipulate the system so that you can give more oral reports. Teach someone to read, which will help your own writing skills.
Poor speaker	Produce written messages where suitable; manipulate the situation so you can offer more written reports. Begin speaking to small groups, starting with as few as two people, take a course, join Toastmasters (see page 165).

CASE #235: CHANGING THE RULES WITH HIGH ENERGY

Many people regard their work as mundane. Suppose you had to explain to a group of salespeople how a credit statement is prepared and used. They probably wouldn't respond with much energy, and as previously explained, your energy could decrease.

Instead of writing a long manual on how to use a credit statement, Sheila Parker produced a snazzy illustration that highlighted the six major points she wanted to make. Then she explained her chart with high energy, using analogies, humor, even short skits.

Parker realized that most people don't want to read instructions and complicated, technical diagrams. She appealed to the right brain by adding high energy in presenting left brain–type information.

Because she changed the rules and displayed creativity and zest where it was unexpected, people began to respond to her presentation.

She was then put in charge of all in-house presentations.

CASE #20: THE OVERCROWDED CLASSROOM

Show me a good professor, and I'll guarantee he brings energy to teaching: energy, ingenuity, and enthusiasm—the elixirs of life. When students say they like to take a professor's class, what are they really saying? He or she is unique, and upbeat, and stimulates my intellect.

I entered the auditorium at the University of Cincinnati to observe Professor William (Bill) McGrane's class Orientation to Business, and I was about to be oriented. More than one thousand students were in attendance, and space limitation had prevented others from signing up.

Music played from large speakers situated throughout, then faded as the class began and Professor McGrane took center stage. Holding a dozen jumping ropes in his hand, he said, "Who wants one?" and eager volunteers ran up to grab the ropes and participate in the first exercise. With the music back on, twelve students jumped to the beat while the others in the audience clapped in unison. Within five minutes this upbeat audience was ready for the lecture series on "How to Market Yourself in the Job Market."

In an environment where learning is seen as a task, cramming for tests exhausting, and contemplating one's future employment frightening, Bill McGrane "changes the rules" and makes learning exciting and educationally enjoyable.

When you bring high energy to a situation where people are not expecting it, you are changing the rules in your favor.

McGrane's main thrust in life is education, and he has found that people of all ages and occupations learn at a more rapid pace when they are encouraged to be creative, enthusiastic, and provocative. Once a month his sessions on building sound self-esteem attract the leaders of corporate America. Contact:

> McGrane Self-Esteem Institute
> 120 East 4th Street
> Cincinnati, Ohio 45202

OPTIMISM AND CHANGING THE RULES

When you review all those things in your life that haven't worked, think again. What difficult lesson did you learn that has utility today?

Like the person who at age twelve hated piano lessons and at 42 loves to play the piano, what did you endure that has become a strength, a blessing, a special ability, an optimistic development?

With a little tolerance and determination the obstacles you face can be your strengths. An optimistic outlook? You bet. A realistic outlook? Most assuredly. It has been said that "man has built most nobly when limitations were greatest." Maybe you can't convert every impediment into a strength, but in an optimistic light consider how you can change the rules to your favor.

Suppose you operate a small market, and your competitor has fourteen stores in your community. His strength may be his proximity to customers in various neighborhoods. How could you meet this challenge? Advertise around town that "if you live within walking distance" to those other stores, "I will deliver for you," "I will pick you up and bring you back." Turn the competitor's advantage into your advantage.

CASE #310: FOURTH IN LINE FOR PROMOTION

Larraine Colter was fourth in line for the job she wanted. Those ahead of her were all capable, and she felt as if the situation was stacked against her. So she listed all of her plusses—character traits, strengths, experiences, relationships—and picked the area where she felt strongest: stamina.

Then she considered other aspects of the job and the work environment. Among the people proceeding up the ladder, one had an MBA, whereas she did not. She decided to work in the office an extra hour beyond what the MBA worked. Later, when the MBA got the job Colter wanted, she successfully sought and became the MBA's assistant.

CASE #179: MASTERING IT ALL

Brian Rissinger worked for a nonprofit, social services organization which operates 12 centers. He has a BA degree in business. Over the years, he rose slowly but steadily by recognizing that the executive director position within the organization was always being filled with someone having a social services background—*not a business background*.

Brian knew that the complexities of running an organization with 12 centers were enormous, and that the potential problem areas were usually interrelated. So this optimistic achiever made himself knowledgeable in the areas of insurance, potential litigation, tax ramifications, and systems management and rose to become the number two man who the various executive directors (always with social services backgrounds) relied upon heavily.

As deputy director, Brian continued to master those areas that other people didn't look into but which were vital to that organization's long-term success. He knew how to purchase supplies at reduced costs, make the buildings more energy efficient, and upgrade the EDP and telecommunications equipment.

Most of the areas in which he became proficient, *originally were not of interest to him*. He became interested because becoming the "resident expert" enabled him to secure a desirable position and income.

Whereas some people see insurance and litigation as boring and uninteresting, Brian approached them with enthusiasm and optimism, *and* his on-the-job expertise could easily be applied in many similar institutions and other businesses.

Brian could have regarded himself in a deadend position with no opportunity for growth or advancement—and received little contention from others. Instead, he created one opportunity after another to increase his value to the organization while employed there.

DISCIPLINE AND CHANGING THE RULES

How well do you handle the things that (at least initially) you don't like to do? A fundamental career rule is that your career must always grow; you cannot coast. Devote a certain amount of time each day or week to professional reading to ensure that you understand new situations and trends. Constantly work to develop your listening skills; it's an area where most people think that they are proficient but are really lacking.

Continually go to seminars; the world is changing too fast to do otherwise.

"Dave, I agree with the need for discipline as discussed, but I don't have time to stay on top of everything."
If you don't have the time, then you lack the discipline. Change the rules to keep pace. Consider something that you would like to accomplish. Before saying you don't have the time, examine what you are doing now. Can any of those things be done simultaneously? What can you let slide or drop? If you commute twenty minutes to work, and your goal is to learn a foreign language, buy a cassette player to use during this time.

If your goal is to read a four-hundred-page book, and you only have ten minutes each night before sleep, set a goal to read three pages nightly.

If you want to read a book on furthering your career, change the rules: Instead of reading from front to back, go to the index or pick some key areas, and read those first (see page 8). Then move forward and back throughout the book. If you're bored right now, go to the index of this book. Find something that appeals to you and devote a few minutes to reading that section.

Within families, a great way to complete a book is to read alternate chapters aloud. A husband and wife, father and son, or two siblings could read alternate chapters and then present the other person with an opinion on the segments covered. This brings families closer, breaks up monotony, and provides a fuller understanding of the material.

Use discipline and change the rules to manage your investments. I have a complex investment program, and I can't monitor each investment daily. So I changed the rules by finding a broker who is able to follow my precise instructions. To simplify my understanding, I maintain a chart of my investments and update it periodically. I use the chart to see when I bought a stock, its "low" and "high," and the last date I checked it. I stay in control.

What charts and graphs can you devise to monitor what otherwise seems cumbersome and time-consuming? Calories consumed? Workouts? Sales progress? Constructing a chart is a discipline. After a while you may need to revise it—more discipline.

> With creativity and ingenuity, you can structure your surroundings to support you.

If you believe you're "stuck" in your office all day, particularly if you eat lunch there and are exposed to idle chatter, a few days a week use a headset and listen to your favorite album. It's enough of a change to help you maintain a healthy balance.

If you dislike standing in a bank line, then bank by mail or have someone else stand in line.

> Within our schedules, our "to-do" lists, the things that we tend to regard as fixed and unchangeable, are actually quite changeable.

CASE #6: DAWN GRAY BLEND

One of the companies I ran during my career was a multistate roofing business with twenty-two branch offices. Lighter colored shingles were becoming popular because they reflected light, although there were many colors available. With twenty-two branch offices, I was concerned about inventory; it's costly to stock twenty colors.

So, I devised a system where one color accounted for ninety percent of our sales. This proved to be a very profitable product that was a practical choice and looked great on homes.

Dawn gray blend included speckles of green, yellow, brown, and red, and yielded several benefits to the purchaser. First, the blend made it difficult to detect defects, dirt, or anything that landed on the roof. Second, if a consumer was having trouble choosing a color, the blend matched many different colors and styles and became a quick and effective choice.

The key to having it work in the business was training the salespeople. As our sales staff became more effective at selling it, the dawn gray blend became often the only color that they would show to prospects. We trained our people to say, "When looking at your house, I think this is the best color." Most people simply did not have a preference.

Eventually the company became the largest residential roofing company in the United States. The cost-effective "one color" program saved customers money because we could buy in great quantities, which added to our profitability. My business could not have grown at the same pace if I had had to maintain substantial roofing inventories.

The key to effectively changing the rules is do it in a manner in which you benefit other people, not hurt them.

EPOD TACTICS

• To improve their cash flow and expand more rapidly, the Marriott Corporation designs, builds, and opens hotels, then syndicates and sells them while maintaining their name on the structure and the right to manage it. They don't own the bricks and mortar, yet they control their use.

• Speed-read your correspondence and use a highlighter. Jot your response directly on the letter, make a copy, and return the letter. It is quick, it is good business, and only those who are highly "protocol" oriented will be offended.

• Instead of turning on the news each morning and hearing

the details of rapes, murders, or fires, play fifteen minutes of a stimulating cassette. Play another fifteen minutes on your way to work, on your way home, and before you go to sleep at night.

• Make a list of those things you do daily. Then review the list. See which activities could be merged, reassigned, reduced, or eliminated.

• Life is a process of continuing growth. With continuing growth comes some pain; you have to be ready for some setbacks in your life, at any stage.

7 Selling

We find our energies are
actually cramped when we are
over-anxious to succeed.
                    —Montaigne

Did they buy or were they sold?

This question can be debated forever without reaching a definitive conclusion. Since when one makes a purchase there is also a sale, we can examine the key elements that go into the buy/sell relationship.

In retailing, as we've seen, the environment created by the retailer can make the customer comfortable. Purchases are made after the customer perceives that the store is reputable, the merchandise is sound, and the sales help is credible. Extensive selling is not that necessary when the environment is conducive to doing business.

In industrial selling the salesperson is often trying to establish or upgrade an account and is competing with an existing, if unknown, supplier. Here, selling often requires prospecting, follow-through, dogged determination, repetitive calls, special deals, and sometimes flamboyant ingenuity.

In either case, where the skill level of your salespeople has been raised by training and supervision, you can achieve increases in volume and profitability.

SELLING: THE CONTEMPORARY SCENE

I have been involved in selling for over forty years and have arrived at the following conclusions.

American selling systems have changed because we became too successful, and the perceived need for improved selling skills diminished.

Many organizations that achieved dominant market share have relaxed their training regimen, and despite their apparent success, the skill level of their salespeople has diminished.

In a growing industry, marginal selling skills may not impede a company's overall growth. But when there is a malfunction or drastic change in the marketplace, such as increased competition or declining demand, the salesperson is unprepared to use the skills necessary to be more competitive and to build a new customer base. What is called selling often is not.

Corporate America seems to be searching for an overly intellectualized concept of sales success. Yet, almost 80 percent of effective sales training consists of instilling the basics on a repetitive and reinforcing basis, including the use of persuasive language.

I have clients who had subjected their salespeople to avant-garde methods of analyzing the social style of prospects, neuro-linguistic programming, and courses in pop psychology. Most salespeople require simple, basic instruction that includes structured sales presentations and presentation books.

After mastering the basics, some salespeople can be encouraged to master more sophisticated processes of inter-personal relations between buyer and seller.

About one fifth of a sales organization produces 50

percent or more of the total volume, on average, and sometimes as high as 80 percent.

Another fifth of the salespeople are constantly battling personal problems, such as divorce, legal problems, chemical dependence; some are lazy and many are mis-hires.

The balance represents 60 percent of the sales organization. They can be stimulated to upgrade their individual skills and thereby add to increased volume and profitability.

Despite these observations, any organization can take simple steps to correct the inequities in their sale systems.

SIX TRUISMS ABOUT SELLING

Here are six provocative statements about selling: (1.) Most people do not like to sell. (2.) Most people do not know how to sell. (3.) As a product or service increases in popularity and use, traditionally the skills of those selling it diminish. (4.) Selling is the least understood function within most companies. (5.) Despite varying degrees of marketing success, many companies are inept in teaching or training salespeople to close. (6.) Whenever an interaction between two or more parties takes place for the purpose of establishing new ideas, exchanging goods or services, or the developing of a relationship, some form of selling will occur and its effectiveness will determine the outcome.

Most people do not like to sell. At seminars, this statement attracts flak like a magnet held over iron filings. Salespeople and managers alike frequently protest; they have much invested in the sales roles they've cultivated. To counter this attitude, I ask pointed questions and request that participants raise their hands.

For example I ask, "Have you ever . . ."

- kept an appointment when the prospect was one hour or more late?

- had a prospect who didn't show at all?
- been allotted half the time you anticipated to make your presentation?
- been promised an order and not gotten it?
- lost an order you were "sure of" to lower prices?
- gotten an order that was turned down by your credit department?
- had a large order cancelled?
- had a customer get upset because of late or incomplete delivery, and take it out on you?
- made a prospecting call in temperatures over 95 or under 30 degrees, or when it was raining or snowing?

None of these occurrences are fun, yet they constitute a major portion of sales activity. Why would most people enjoy that part of the role? Generally, they don't.

Getting the order, getting paid on an account, winning a sales contest are the enjoyable parts of selling, yet they represent a relatively small part of a salesperson's time and activity. Once a manager recognizes the indisputable truth that most people do not like to sell, there is a greater possibility of dealing openly and effectively with the sales personnel.

The most disciplined salespeople achieve the greatest earnings, because they know that calling on prospects, staying organized, traveling long distances, having orders canceled, having appointments canceled, facing the possibility of rejection, and overcoming objections are steps in the process that lead to sales success.

CO-COMMUNICATION: A KEY SELLING TOOL INCORPORATING EPOD

Let's examine the effective use of language in selling. When you ask, "Do you have digital watches?" the typical undisciplined response of sales help is to say, "We have all kinds of digital watches." The disciplined salesperson who is skilled in using a technique called co-communication recognizes that saying we have every kind of watch does not serve the customer because it does not address his specific needs.

Any salesperson can immediately become more effective by using co-communication. Co-communication means encouraging another person (a customer) to talk about him or herself, his or her needs, values, likes, dislikes, goals, and feelings.

Co-communication is both a powerful and essential tool in your company's success. When you use co-communication to ask the right questions, the customer will actually tell you how to handle the sale. With this knowledge, you can better serve prospects and turn them into buyers. Co-communication helps answer two essential questions: What is the customer really interested in? What will make him want to buy?

It enables you to dig beneath the prospect's words ("I can't afford it," "We're happy with our current supplier") and find out what will really move the prospect, turn him or her on, make the customer want to buy.

The following statement reflects the customer's goals, values, and feelings. "Your price is too high." But how can you determine what the customer means—what lies behind those words.

Using co-communication, you would ask, "Why do you say that?" Each question you ask is designed to obtain more information about what the prospect means. Other responses that you could offer include: *What did you have in mind? Why do you feel that way? What gives rise to that opinion? Run that by me one more time!*

In co-communication you answer questions, or address statements, with questions, to obtain more precise information about what the customer is saying. When a customer says, "Your price is too high," what does that really mean? There are dozens of reasons for making the statement, and only two of them directly deal with price. Most of the reasons represent tactics the customer is using (for example, some customers have learned to automatically cringe when a price is mentioned) or a condition the customer must have fulfilled before buying.

When you respond to "Your price is too high" with "Why do you say that?" the customer then redefines his or her answer. Below are the most likely responses and the possible purpose behind each one.

Response	Intent
"Because we're buying something similar for less."	Convince me yours is worth the difference.
"Everyone gives discounts."	A test, a trial for a better deal.
"I hadn't seen this model before."	Needs more information or verification.
"It's a lot more than we intended to spend."	Needs convincing to upgrade.
"It's over our budget."	A test to gauge your response.
"My authorization is limited."	No authority to buy above $X.
"We like yours better, but we've got a lower price."	Wants to negotiate.
"My friend who bought something similar last year for less."	Outdated information.
"We'll wait for prices to come down."	Procrastination.
"We can get it for less."	A test to see if you'll drop the price.

Without co-communication dialogue, the statement "your price is too high" can be interpreted only from your viewpoint. There are between 350,000 and 500,000 words in the English language, and most people use only 2 to 3 percent of them. Even the more common words have several connotations. It stands to reason that statements may have veiled intents.

Once the customer is questioned using co-communication and offers a new response, you derive greater understanding of the prospect's values, goals, and feelings. You can then pose another question to the prospect's response to gain even greater insight as to how to serve him or her. At any time during a customer encounter the golden rule is

When in doubt, ask another question.

Co-communication always prompts prospects to tell you how to sell them; there need be no misunderstandings. If you aren't certain about something a prospect says, you ask about it to make sure you fully understand.

How do the EPOD elements apply to co-communication? Use energy to get undivided attention? Use persuasiveness to find out what the other party needs. Use optimism to convey a warm positive feeling. Use discipline to speak at appropriate moments, to give the customer a chance to respond or say more, to ask another question at the appropriate time.

Selling is so much more than telling. Most sales training still focuses on transferring company and product or service information to the customer in the shortest time and in the most effective form, nodding affirmatively for a while when the customer speaks, then proceeding to close. Selling is often approached as a sales pitch, and companies place a high value on the verbal skills of their salespeople.

Armed with this training, sales representatives experience careers marked by up and down performance, supposedly controlled by the market or the season. These salespeople and the managers who supervise them don't understand why they achieve uneven results; it may actually be poor use of language that's choking their effectiveness.

CASE #23: BASIC CO-COMMUNICATION QUESTIONS

My wife and I were shopping for a new home in the Northern Virginia suburbs of Washington, D.C. The market had been escalating for fifteen years and was reputed to be the third costliest residential real estate market in the nation. Homes of all styles and price ranges were selling quickly. Even homes constructed with mediocre craftsmanship sold at relatively high prices.

We spent numerous weekends attending the open houses of homes in the high six-figure range. We met and dealt with a variety of real estate salespeople, many in sales for more than ten years. Yet we were seldom asked any of the basic questions—fact-finding questions—that are crucial to effective selling.

Here are some basic questions each agent could have asked: What is you name, address, and phone number? (Needed for follow-up, but this was not evident to most of the agents we met.) Where do you live now? Why are you thinking of moving? How long have you been at you present residence? How many people are there in your household? How many rooms and baths do you want or need? How important is it for you to be near your business, school, shopping, airports? How long have you looked for a home? What kinds and styles of homes have you seen?

These are basic questions, which were not asked by a surprising number of agents and brokers with whom we spoke. Hence, co-communication could not be used. Using co-communication, the agents could have asked the following types of questions to draw us out—learn about our aspirations and feelings—and thereby help both buyer and seller consumate a sale: Do you have a picture of your current home (or could we visit there)? What do you like most (and least) about your current home? What are your three primary reasons for shopping for a new home? (Only one may be needed.) What are the three primary considerations for your new home? What are three secondary considerations for your new home?

When answered, these qualifying questions would have benefited both buyer and seller. The agent would have had immediate access to our goals, values, and desires. We could have reduced the endless trips to houses not meeting our specifications.

Even when we volunteered the information that we wanted the salespeople to have, it did not seem to affect their desire to show us what *they* thought we should buy. Here is a sampling of the agents' statements to us: "Here is a home I just love." "I think this one is a real (bargain, beauty, steal)." "This one really grows on you." "Let's look at this and see if you'd like to make an offer." "This one has been on the market for a while, so they may be open to an offer."

Many agents told us how successful their companies were and how many awards they had won. How tough is it to be a million-dollar producer when the average house sells for six figures?

One must be licensed to sell real estate, yet most of those who complete the training and testing are never successful. Most agents simply jump from territory to territory, or project to project, in an effort to stay with whatever seems hot. Those who are successful usually have upgraded their skills.

Salespeople who do not use co-communication have usually made an early determination (sometimes based on their experience) as to what the prospect means. If their judgment is faulty, and it frequently is, a breakdown in communication occurs, which results in a "no-sale."

The trap in answering a question with an answer is that you will tend to use *your own value system* as a measurement, and unless your value system is the same as the prospect's, there is a malfunction in your communication. For example: If the prospect says, "Which of these are the best?" and the salesperson says, "Here is the one I like," the salesperson is operating from his or her own value system.

NOT TO PICK ON THE U.S. AUTO INDUSTRY, BUT . . .

I do a lot of business within the automotive industry. I enjoy the people in the industry, my earnings, and the challenges that I face. The automobile industry, however, often uses antiquated techniques when it comes to selling. Today, the vast majority of automobile sales representatives still see each customer as a one-shot deal. Yet the young man or woman who walks into the showroom is going to buy eight or ten cars over the next twenty or thirty years and represents $140,000 in purchases, including new autos, parts, and services.

CASE #11: WORKING IN THE "ZONE"

My wife and I were shopping for a new Audi. On a Friday evening, about three miles from our home, we visited a dealership which displayed Audis, Porsches, and Mercedes. The showroom was a large, lavish, multimillion-dollar structure with an art gallery on one of its levels. The cars were all waxed to a high luster and beautifully displayed.

We spent about twenty minutes looking at the various cars, but no sales representative approached us. We decided to find help. I saw a man leaning on the balcony above the display area. I indicated that if he were an employee, I would like to speak to him. He motioned for me to come upstairs. So I did. Here is our conversation:

SALES MANAGER: What can I do for you?

ME: Do you work here?

SM: I'm the sales manager here. (No name.)

ME: Great, because I'm looking to buy a car.

SM: Well, that's the business we're in.

ME: I wasn't sure.

SM: Why . . . what . . . I don't understand.

ME: My wife and I have been looking at your cars for about twenty minutes and no salespeople approached us.

SM: I see.

ME: There seem to be quite a few people in those little offices downstairs.

SM: Yes, those are our salespeople.

ME: I'm wondering why none of them came over to speak to us.

SM: Well, what kind of car were you looking for?

ME: An Audi.

SM: That's easy to explain. Most of those salespeople are Porsche and Mercedes salespeople.

ME: Great . . . Now tell me . . . how did they know what kind of car I was looking for?

He assured me they were interested in our business. He asked us to stand near the Audi in the center of the showroom, and he would send a salesperson to help. Minutes later, we were approached by a neat, well-dressed young man.

He introduced himself, apologized for our inconvenience, and then uttered the four most unproductive words in retailing: "May I help you?" From that point, it was downhill as far as his sales skills were concerned. Immediately, he waxed enthusiasticly to me about Audi's great mileage, its comfort for someone who spent a lot of time commuting, and how it had all the features of larger, so-called luxury cars. He was only slightly abashed when told that the car was for my wife (a noncommuter).

Without a break in his speech, he then directed his attention to selling my wife this car. He never asked what she was presently driving (an Audi). He did not seek to know if she had driven this model before (she had). In fact, she had owned two Audis previously and had shopped for and driven this very model elsewhere. Can you see the information opportunities missed?

The salesman opened the hood and elaborated on the five-cylinder overhead "cam" engine. I was impressed. I thought they had to have an equal number of cylinders, such as four, six, or eight. He commented on the superiority of the braking system and how the Germans had that department down pat, far ahead of American manufacturers.

Finally, he invited us to his office. For the next ten minutes he discussed how their dealership was number two in Audi sales on the East Coast and how he knew this was the best dealer. After I suggested it he had our car appraised, then told us the cost of a new Audi with ours as a trade-in. He told us we could probably get an Audi for less elsewhere but not from such a great dealer. They didn't have to give large discounts, because they were number two.

We thanked him for his time. I gave him my business card, which was only fair since he had given me his. The next day, we bought an Audi at the same price from a dealer eighteen miles from our home. The whole time, the first salesman had never asked our names, nor had he asked whom the car was for, if we had ever owned or driven an Audi, how long we had owned our Audi, what we liked about our last Audi, what we would like in a new one, how familiar we were with the new model, how many miles the car would be driven annually, if it would be used for business, the number of children in our family.

Why didn't he ask us any of the above questions? The answer, in all probability, is one or more of the following: He didn't think of it; he hadn't been trained; or worse, he didn't care.

How well did this manager and salesman interact with my wife and me, based on the EPOD Theory? The energy conveyed to us was moderate to low. The persuasiveness was nonexistent. There was some optimism, for example, they had pride in their zone and the quality of the vehicles they were selling, but it was only optimism for what they wanted to sell, not for what our needs were.

How about the discipline factor? They did poorly on the basics. Combined with the poor performance in the other three areas, this made the probability of being successful, in other words, making the sale, very low.

The automobile industry represents an integral part of our economy. When auto sales suffer, our gross national product suffers drastically. Despite the number of foreign cars sold in the United States, our automobile industry now produces a fine product.

The problem may be that the public doesn't perceive it as such.

Many automobile dealers have improved their once impractical attitudes about service and have created strong profit centers in their parts and service departments. The entire industry made a quantum leap forward when it supported ASTN (Automotive Satellite Television Network).

On this private network, dealers tune in daily to programming. They hear about such issues as new services, products, and methods; improvements in communication; and hiring and training for sales, service, and administrative personnel.

This powerful idea has not been endorsed by every automobile dealer, yet it is available on a very practical basis. Probably those that need it most seek it least. The banking and hotel industries need similar programs.

The next time you shop for an automobile, grade the salesperson and see if he or she is using persuasive, high-energy techniques before you decide to give the dealer your money. If the techniques are not working on the salesroom floor, they may be equally absent in the service department.

CASE #77: RESISTANCE TO CO-COMMUNICATION LANGUAGE

I was conducting a seminar for engineers who specify and design a product sold by an industrial sales organization. When I presented the idea of co-communication, there was immediate resistance. A sales engineer who was particularly vocal wanted to know "How can I, as an engineer who is supposed to know my product, respond to another engineer with questions like 'Why do you ask?' I think I would look foolish." He had answered his own question: If the method would make him feel foolish, there might be a good reason not to use it.

In that training session, we suggested that the co-communication questions be written by each salesperson (in their own handwriting) on a series of three-by-five cards. The vocal sales engineer agreed to participate in using the system for twenty one days only—accepting the early awkwardness, putting aside the ego problem of feeling foolish, and using the cards as reminders and cues. The sales team agreed to measure their effectiveness, at the end of twenty one days, based on improved communications and increased sales activity.

Sixty days later we asked for and received a completed

questionnaire from each participant. Based on their reporting, only 78 percent attempted the process at least once. Of those who attempted the process at least once, only 40 percent used it for two weeks or more. Twenty three percent experienced improved communications and felt it was contributing positively to their sales activity.

Most of the 23 percent were still using it at the time of the follow-up seminar. Best of all, the general manager of the division who had attended the earlier meeting used the practice during union negotiations with favorable results. A majority of people are reluctant to try new training ideas, but those who can quickly pass through the awkward stage.

Co-communication remains one of the most powerful techniques we use in training. Yet, without spaced repetition and the support of those charged with follow-through training or field management, this great method does not become a working tool for salespeople.

THE ACID TEST

The use of the acronym ACID can help you improve your communication. By remembering the four letters A,C,I,D you have an easy way to remember the steps to positive, powerful communication: A (arouse), C (cultivate), I (information), D (determine).

If you can arouse a prospect sufficiently, then you can cultivate his or her interest, and the prospect will likely offer information that will help you to determine how to deal with him or her. If you and the prospect communicate well and there are no misunderstandings in your communication, it is because you are talking about things that interest the prospect, such as his or her own goals and values.

Most people reverse the ACID process and start with the D, by first making a determination about you—about how you look, by what you have said, by how you are standing, and other cues.

Did they buy or were they sold? Examine how ACID

works in selling and how you know if you are communicating effectively with a prospect.

A sales presentation that is tailored to a prospect's needs, goals, values, and feelings is viewed more favorably by the prospect than one which is not. If you ask a friend where he bought his new suit, he will usually reply "I bought it at X," or "I bought it from Y." He is claiming credit for the purchase. He's not likely to say, "So and so sold it to me," in which case credit for the transaction goes to the seller.

This is more than a play on words, it reveals the customer's perception of a transaction and, possibly, the skills of the seller.

Using the ACID technique enables the salesperson to make the customer feel he "bought," not as if he "was sold."

Arouse. Did you arouse sufficient interest in the prospect and give him encouragement to spend more time with your idea or product? The outcome of most buy-sell relationships is based on what happens in the first two minutes in person, and in the first thirty seconds over the phone.

Cultivate. Did you cultivate the prospect's interest? Did you ask questions (co-communication) to induce the prospect to talk about him or herself—goals, values, and feelings?

Information. Did you get sufficient information, and how did you remember it? Did you use the information to lead to additional questioning which produced more information? If you make multiple calls prior to attempting to sell or close, how and where did you file the information?

Determine. Did you determine from the information on hand how, when, and where you would make your presentation, what the prospect's goals, values, and needs were, and how you would fulfill them with your presentation?

Let me arouse a person, cultivate him or her, and that person will give me the information that I need and that will help me determine how he or she would like to be dealt with.

There are essentially four motivational environments in which decisions are made: gain, pride, fear, and imitation. Perhaps these are not the noblest of motivations but, being human, our decision-making process often boils down to What do I get out of it? How does it make me look? What will happen if I don't do it? Who else is doing it?

If I'm trying to sell to people, I don't have the right to judge them. To be successful, however, I have to get as close as possible to standing in their shoes. I do this by asking them how they feel, and I listen. I don't make any value judgments, which helps me to set up an environment where they feel comfortable. While I cannot motivate everyone into doing anything at anytime, I can support an environment in which motivation may occur.

EPOD TACTICS

• I am glad to live in a society of aggressive selling. Most people would not like to make decisions about new products or ideas on their own. It takes someone to convince them.

• Sell more (and more per customer). Suppose you run a shoe store and traditionally one out of five people in the store end up buying a pair of shoes. If you sell one out of four people, you capture 25 percent rather than 20 percent of the prospects.

If you find it difficult to improve on long-standing customer capture rates, consider what would happen if you were able to sell an average of 1.5 pairs per one out of five customers.

• Creative selling comes about when the buyer is convinced it is his decision to buy. Notice that the satisfied customer often says, "I bought it from . . .," and seldom, ". . . sold it to me."

• It is not the purpose of advertising to be an art form which we stand around and admire. Sound advertising *sells* a product or service.

- Acknowledge that the power of an idea can be measured by the degree of resistance that it encounters.
- Are you willing to write down the ideas that you don't agree with and that don't fit your own value system? As you read this or any other book, list those ideas you are resisting rather than the ones with which you agree.
- Take the most compelling idea you listed and share it with a half dozen people. Do they like the idea, will they use it, and when? You'll quickly see why it is difficult to sell ideas.
- Some companies won't use an idea because it comes from an outside source. To sell ideas to people, get them to see it as theirs. This is not deception, but an effective form of packaging the idea, using persuasive language and discipline.

When presenting ideas to clients, I use a resistance reducing format: "Bob, I saw your staff doing something, and it struck me that with one little modification it could really pay off. Let me tell you what it is." This technique integrates my idea with something that they are already doing.

- Take time to find out about or understand the value system of the other person.
- Send two inexpensive reminder gifts annually to clients, customers, and friends. Please note that many companies discourage or prohibit employees from receiving gifts, so make it simple, thoughtful, and unique.
- If you want to sell something other than by its "low price," make an inventory of all things surrounding your product or service, and the people and equipment needed to support the product.
- Get to know this inventory and present it as part of your package before you quote the price. It reduces the perception of a higher price. Your price appears lower.
- Closing the sale is the natural conclusion of successfully completing each step of the selling plan.
- To improve communication remember the following:
  1. Answer questions with questions.

2. Objections are a sign of interest.
3. The degree of intensity given to the objection measures the degree of its importance.
4. The power of an idea can be measured by the degree of resistance it attracts.
5. Technical questions do not always require technical answers.

• The next time you decide to market a "low price" product or service that depends on volume, remember these three realities:

1. Someone will always have a lower price.
2. There will always be price objections.
3. You will lose some orders to a lower price.

• I advise every high school or college student to experience door-to-door selling. There is no better way to build self-confidence and find out what the real world of buying and selling is all about.

8 Negotiating Agreements and Retaining Outside Advisors

He that complies against
his will is of his own
opinion still.
— Samuel Butler

Growing up, I tried everything at one time or another: I manipulated, connived, brawled, and was deceitful. The one saving grace was inheriting my grandfather's values. I learned important principles by observing him. Although he could neither read nor write, he lived by very simple rules, and I believe if all negotiating and contracting carried this preface there would be fewer breakdowns in relationships—I know for sure that there would be less litigation.

- Never give your word unless you mean it.
- Never shake on a deal unless you intend to fulfill your part.
- If it ain't yours, don't touch it. (If I found something in the street, my grandfather insisted that I leave it alone or turn it in to a third party.)

"Those were fine principles years ago, Dave, but today it's everyone for himself. You'd better grab what you can while you can."

You can operate that way, but you will always find people who can grab more and are tougher than you. You will constantly be wondering if the next guy will take advantage of you.

A CONTRACT IS A CONTRACT

A young athlete signs with a major sports franchise. His agent negotiates a three-year contract stating how the athlete will be paid and that, in turn, he will give his best effort. The athlete has a better year than anticipated, so his agent says, "You are worth more than we bargained for. Don't report to training camp. Hold out."

Is this justified because no one knew at the time that the athlete was going to be great? Is he entitled to more?

What does a contract mean? Essentially it means you give your word. Most breakdowns in contract relations are based on the integrity level of the negotiating parties. To improve the outcome of your contracting requires being clear about with whom you are doing business, what each side wants, and what each side anticipates.

AN OATH IS AN OATH. During the Reagan Administration, there were more than one hundred public servants investigated or indicted for malfeasance. Each took an oath to represent us and our best interests. Yet even the Attorney General proclaimed he had done nothing illegal—unethical maybe, but not illegal.

A judge once told me that the courts do not decide on issues of ethics or morality. He was, of course, correct. However, I am not so sure that that was our founding fathers' intent in the original construction of our laws, and it may be a key ingredient as to why our legal system is breaking down.

When you leave morality and ethics out of your negotiations, most contracts and the relationships of the parties involved fail.

IN BUSINESS, TO EXPLOIT IS TO LOSE

I have many opportunities each year to take advantage of people when I negotiate. Because of my experience I can predetermine how to structure a deal that turns out to be highly favorable to me and not so favorable to the other person.

When you enter into agreements that do not benefit both parties, ultimately the other party is going to be unhappy and may begin to dishonor parts of the agreement. Then no one benefits.

When you negotiate to get your best deal to the detriment of the other party, the agreement is ultimately going to fail.

If I lease space to you, or I sell you something under terms and conditions that are biased against you or overly burdensome, eventually you will find a way to circumvent our agreement.

CASE #67: INTOXICATING NEGOTIATIONS

Years back, I had a business associate who always set up meetings with vendors at a posh restaurant. Dinner would be followed by considerable drinking. A nondrinker himself, his strategy was to get the other party inebriated so that when we began negotiating terms, they would give away the store.

I participated in these dinner meetings a couple of times but felt uncomfortable with vendors on their third or fourth martini. I didn't want or need this type of negotiating advantage. If I were to take it, what would that say about the long-term health of my business and about me?

These vendors found it profitable to sell to me. I didn't know anything about their personal lives, but they were basically good people. I didn't need to wring them dry for every favorable term I could get. How would they feel about that down the pike?

> When you deal with the other party in mind, you are transmitting a message to them that how they fare is as important to you as how you fare in this relationship, and you get a stronger agreement from the standpoint of both parties honoring it over the long run.

CASE #33: GIVE AND TAKE

My company had an annual contract with the Lloyd A. Fry Company to purchase materials from them at an agreed upon cost. (The company has since been sold to Owens-Corning.) We were one of their largest customers. Five months into the contract, their vice president, Woody Woodward, asked to meet me in Pittsburgh to discuss something important.

I arrived the evening before and met him for breakfast the next morning. I knew what was on his mind. He said, "We've looked at our existing contract with you and found that we really can't make it for the price per unit that we offered you."

I could essentially have said to him, "You made your bed, now lie in it, we'll talk in seven months." He would have still supplied me but would have been unhappy about it. I could have said, "Okay, you've pushed me over a barrel, but just remember, you owe me. Right?"

My business was growing, and I wanted to have a solid, long-term relationship with this important supplier. So I said, "Tell me the amount you have to have to make it." He said, "Twenty cents per unit," and explained the reasoning behind this request. I picked up a pad and wrote down some figures—I already knew what I was going to do. I said, "I'll give you twenty-five cents."

He was taken aback. "Wait a second, I said I only needed twenty cents."

I said, "I know, I'm offering twenty-five."

He said, "Why?"

I said, "Tell me how much time that buys me."

He said, "Three years."

I got a long-term commitment and he got an excellent price. When he reported to his president, a tough son-of-a-gun, I knew that Woodward could play the hero. I could almost hear the words in their conference room, "If Yoho is willing to offer us five cents more when we didn't ask for it, he's got to be for real."

What does Woodward remember about our negotiation? That in a moment of need I was not only fair, I was generous. In turn, he became generous with me, and I never had a problem with him.

CASE #37: YOU GIVE IN, YOU GET

Another time, one of my companies was providing services to homes damaged by hailstorms. Homeowners called us for estimates and gave the information to their insurance companies. Then we were contacted by an insurance adjustor who represented several different insurance companies.

One of my managers called me and said, "This one insurance adjustor is out to break our back. He's nickel-and-diming on every contract we've written." I said, "This is an emotional, not a practical, issue. I want you to call the adjustor and tell him, 'We finished the latest job using 6 percent less material than anticipated. Should I wait for the remittance and resubmit, or can it be adjusted now?' Work it out as well as you can and call me," I finished telling him.

Guess what happened? The next two dozen times we dealt with that adjustor, he eased up on us. He had a strong need to prove that he was right, and when we voluntarily adjusted downward it was the same as affirming him. He had less need to "get" us.

RECOGNIZING VALUE SYSTEMS IN NEGOTIATING

Everyone whom you encounter has a value system, which is detectable if you observe the person long enough. When someone questions your price, you may think he is reflecting a value system, but often it is a tactic.

If the person with whom you are negotiating has an expensive watch or furnishings or a high-priced automobile, you are getting a glimpse of a value system, though that doesn't mean they would not attempt to buy these things at the best price. The customer wearing a Rolex watch may have determined to get the top-of-the-line instrument because he placed a high value on style, looks, prestige, and so on. If price, not value, were the real issue, he would be wearing a ten-dollar digital watch.

Values are established by listening carefully to responses when you negotiate. What may seem like simple social conversation has great impact on what you will say next.

Whenever I present a negotiated agreement I do so only after identifying someone's value system. Then I make my presentation in accordance with it.

A caveat: An established, irrefutable fact about negotiation is that if the other person places a low value on truth, ethics, or integrity, your negotiation will have little meaning, no matter what form it takes, and you will be in for disappointing consequences.

CASE #98: THE SPOKEN WORD TAKES PRECEDENCE

I originally met Mel Rosenblatt just after he had become the new vice president of sales for a large but struggling company. High volume and low profitability had his company on the ropes. He sought my company's account because we would be one of his largest customers.

After we became his customer, we began negotiating on little more than a handshake and four paragraphs in a letter. This letter would determine our annual relationship. When conditions arose that had to be addressed, we were always able to handle them by phone. I never once had a falling out, disagreement, or condition wherein I felt he went back on his word.

Over the past thirty years our relationship has shifted. He is a client today with a different company in a different industry. Everyone who knows Rosenblatt marvels at the ease with which he keeps his word. I've learned that his reputation is the means by which he negotiates for new business and retains old customers.

I have negotiated long and complex situations with him involving great sums in the span of ten minutes on the telephone. My degree of trust in him is so great that I would play poker with him over the phone.

A PLACE FOR HONEST NEGOTIATIONS AND AGREEMENTS

If honesty is important to you, you don't need to declare it. Simply practice being honest. You say, "Forget it, because the world is basically dishonest?" Yes, our value system in the United States has changed over the years, and being honest won't increase your probability of encountering other honest people.

There is a place, however, for honest people, people who protect the property of others, people who become honest cogs in large organizations. You c̶ . . . . with the rest of the crowd. It isn't . . .

"But, Dave, why stick my neck out fo . . . less people care about anyways?"

If that's your attitude, then there is . . . that you will be a high achiever. Mair . . . adopting peer group values, or rati . . . mediocre career and life.

Most of the achievers I know . . . establish a set of values from whicl . . .

CASE #302: A QUESTION OF VALUES

We had a group of licensees who bought their supplies from the company we cited as the "recommended supplier." A man visiting my office wanted his company to be cited as the recommended supplier; he was a direct competitor to our existing supplier. I told him that we were not interested, we already had a fine relationship, we saw no reason to change, and contractually we couldn't change.

My visitor quietly pointed out how his company offered lower prices for some goods and how their delivery terms and service were superior in some areas. I said that these items were nice but that I honored my existing agreements and relationships.

Then he asked me, "What will it take to make a deal?" I said, "Sorry." He said, "If you allow us to be the recommended supplier, it will be profitable to your company, and it could be profitable to you personally." I said, "In what way?" He suggested a deal involving payments to me under the table. He said that they would be untraceable cash payments.

I thought about his offer for a moment before I said, "How secure would you be with our relationship?" If I were to accept this offer, then I would be prey to the next offer, and the next. My own set of values would go out the window. I could have used the money—twenty thousand or thirty thousand dollars a year was a sizable sum back then. But to pervert my value system for that? It doesn't make sense.

"Wait a minute, Dave, that ain't the way life works."

Yes, and that's why we have the Ivan Boeskys who end up behind bars. People who hold positions of high responsibility in government and in corporations, who pervert their value systems, receive at best, temporary monetary gain.

The world is full of people who diverted funds, perhaps early in their careers, and went on to become very successful, only to have the earlier transgression exposed and watch everything come tumbling down.

Some entrepreneurs structure their businesses to steal cash from them. I'm not trying to be holier than thou—realistically, the risk of diversion of funds is simply too great. Do you want to play games with your financial statements and wait for the IRS to knock on your door? Are you going to surrender a part of your life for hot cash when there are many better ways to honestly earn a dollar?

Why go to sleep each night wondering if tomorrow is the day you are going to be exposed? No size kickback is worth the disruption of your value system and peace of mind.

FRAUD IS NEVER WORTH THE PRICE

A businessman who pleaded guilty to defrauding the government once ran a full-page ad in *The Philadelphia Inquirer* titled "An Open Letter of Apology." In it, he noted that he had lost his business, health, and family as a result of his offense.

He urged others to learn a lesson from his mistakes. "Don't make the almighty dollar the guiding force for your business decisions," he said. "Instead, for every business decision you make, ask yourself: is what I am doing right?"

He closed with this message for young people considering business careers: "The true measure of success is not your financial worth, but how much you are worth to your friends, family, community and most of all to yourself. Right now I don't feel like I'm worth very much."

Communication Briefings, © 1988.
Reprinted with permission

STRUCTURING YOUR OWN AGREEMENTS

Many agreements can be expressed without legal assistance. Once again, this requires personal discipline. I create most of my agreements on my own letterhead—not legal-sized stationery—using simple, nurturing language generally not subject to misinterpretation.

I ask the other party to review the document in detail and see if the agreement is in their best interest. If they want to have a legal advisor review it, I say fine. I do not advocate, however, that they seek business advice from or have the agreement structured by an attorney. You don't need fifteen paragraphs for what can be said effectively in fifty words.

Confusing language that must be reinterpreted is to no one's benefit except the lawyer's.

If you do not understand every clause in any agreement that you are considering, don't sign it.

Many people believe lawyers are necessary for contracts because they provide assurance, which is an invalid assumption. I go to my legal advisor after I devise an agreement or contract. I ask what it might lead to, how it might be interpreted, what I might also include, and that's it.

Frequently when I submit a proposed agreement to someone, that person will take my document to his or her lawyer. Invariably, we have to explain the conditions to the lawyer, extend the length of agreement, and revise the ideas that we originally agreed upon. Obviously our cost increases.

Your ability to have a satisfactory contractual relationship is directly related to the length of the contract.

The longer the agreement, the less probable that you will have a viable, long-term relationship.

While all of the important issues have to be covered, when an agreement gets too long, it is usually because someone is trying to obscure the terms of the relationship.

The preamble to any agreement can be simply stated: "Party A and Party B are entering into this agreement with this intent. Here is the intent of Party A. Here is the intent of Party B. In the event of dispute, here is how Party A and Party B will solve it."

Contracts between most parties need not be more than three to five pages. Always look for what you can take out of agreements, not add. The responsibility of both parties is how to keep the agreement simple and to the point.

CASE #25: TOO LONG MEANS THINGS WILL GO WRONG

Once when I was seeking to buy a sizable business, which in itself is a tricky proposition, I was faced with an overly long lease. In this small, closely held business, the president of the company owned the building in his own name and leased the premises back to the business.

The negotiations had gone on for months. Closing day was held on a Saturday as a convenience to me because I was returning from out of town. My attorney came several hours before I was scheduled to arrive with a sizable deposit.

The lease provisions consisted of thirty-two pages! My attorney highlighted all the clauses and phrases of concern to us. (I found out later that the parties assembled that morning had spent hours just on the lease provisions.) I had expected to close quickly, but this was not the case.

I asked to review the lease, which required about forty-five minutes, and then asked the seller's attorney why it was so complicated. Here is our conversation:

ATTY: It's a standard lease that we draw up.
ME: Let me see the lease they used previously.
ATTY: We can't do that.
ME: They had to have the same protection that we want, so let's use that lease.
ATTY: Sorry, we can't.
ME: Well, just tell me, how long was that lease?
ATTY: I don't remember.
ME: Was it twenty or thirty pages?
ATTY: No, I don't think so.
ME: Why does this have thirty-two pages?
ATTY: You are going to be taking over their building. I advised several protections.

I reminded the attorney that when we negotiated for the deal, we were aware of this lease-back arrangement. In fact, we had offered to buy the building. He wouldn't budge. I said, "I don't think we're going to proceed with the deal. There are clauses here that I can't live with—these were not part of the negotiations."

He said, "I am representing my client, and this is what I advise him to do." I said, "Fine, but we're not doing business. Anything that takes thirty-two pages is not in my best interest. We haven't even moved into the building, and there could be unforeseen problems."

The attorney got flushed and said, "Mr. Yoho, you are petulant." I said to him, "That may be, but I've learned that if an agreement becomes burdensome at the outset, it's only going to get worse later."

The Declaration of Independence is a short document developed by many people with clarity and thoughtfulness. It created an independent country—and it didn't take thirty-two pages.

DON'T BE INTIMIDATED AT REAL ESTATE CLOSINGS. When you purchase real estate, you are besieged with fifteen or twenty documents involving dozens of clauses. The typical person will not completely read all these documents. I read every document. I request a copy of all documents in advance of the closing. If I don't receive them, I read them at the closing.

It takes time to understand the terms so that you can buy a piece of property and sign the appropriate documents with intelligence.

If there is a clause I don't understand or that I disagree with, I won't sign it until the modification is made.

"But, Dave, what if it takes several hours to read these documents. How can you make the time for such matters?"

How better could you be spending your time than

carefully reviewing the terms of contracts you are about to sign? How important is it for you to understand and confirm the purchases, sales, or relationships that you enter into in your life?

THE KEYS TO WORKING WITH LAWYERS, ACCOUNTANTS, AND CONSULTANTS

My grandmother was from Estonia, and from her I learned an old Baltic curse: "May your life be filled with lawyers." We have become a litigious society. There are nearly seven hundred thousand lawyers in the United States and projections of one million within five years. This equates to one lawyer for every 250 adults. Japan, with a population of 125 million people, roughly half of the United States, has only 110,000 lawyers.

The lawyer glut contributes to a situation where they reach for business, and this creates an atmosphere of fear, distrust, and an abdication of sound ethics and morals in our business and personal life. I've learned that if you can avoid taking business advice from lawyers, you are going to be better off. Certainly we need legal advice. However, working with or through lawyers, one often notices a working style that leads to confrontation, abuse of your time, energy, and funds. Cases are extended, troubles are manufactured, and things become much more complicated than they need to be. I advise clients to

- Shop for an attorney who meets your needs.
- Check their references. Ask to speak to bankers, landlords, and suppliers. Check them out the same as with any vendor.
- Check on their specialties. You may be better off working with three or four small firms rather than one large one.

- Ask for complete information on fees and other pricing factors, and get it in writing if possible.
- Ask for the names of previous clients, and call them. Ask for details such as promptness, courtesy, follow-through, how the services were used, level of satisfaction, and would they use them again. (Bear in mind that you probably won't be given the names of "problem" clients.)
- Evaluate how the attorney asks questions of you and what he feels is important to know about you and your business.

USING ATTORNEYS IN YOUR BEST INTEREST

While a high percentage of the advice that small business entrepreneurs receive from lawyers and accountants is not in their best interest, often it is because the entrepreneur is holding back information.

You are responsible also for maintaining goals, acknowledging changes that occur, and coming up with the effective decisions—not your retained counsel. Too often when entrepreneurs take a deal or a proposed strategy to counsel, they unwittingly engage in deal breaking rather than deal making. The counsel, who may not know all the facts, tells you not to proceed, even though you think that you should.

Give the professional all of the relevant information if you want his best advice.

At the same time, don't use the professional as a whipping boy. Many people wait until a situation develops then sours, and say, "Well, he told me to do it, and that's where I went wrong." Decisions are ultimately yours, and as you become responsible for them, you will feel satisfied about the decisions you make. I tell all my clients to be responsible for their own actions and to know what their risk is.

CASE #14: NOT COMMUNICATING LEGALESE

Joseph Lyman is a Washington, D.C., attorney who represents large and small businesses with special tax situations or complications. His clients are frequently those who are having problems with the Federal Trade Commission or wage and hours laws, and he has become a specialist representing companies who treat their sales associates as independent contractors.

I met Joe when we were each making a speech at a convention for contractors in the building material industry and was struck by his ability to relate to the contractors, and their ability, in turn, to relate to him. I assumed that he specialized in that industry. When his speech ended, the attendees crowded around him asking for his card and feeding him endless questions. Heading out the door, others commented on Joe's techniques and asked for his card.

Later, I found out that his practice represented dozens of industries such as cosmetics, real estate, fisheries, land development, and food and beverage, and that he has developed the same excellent rapport with each group.

I asked him how he knew so much about each of these industries and where he developed his speaking techniques. He said that in each case, he researched the industry, attended local meetings, met and interviewed prominent members, and read everything about the particular industry he could.

When he made a speech, he avoided using "lawyer talk" and legal language. Instead, he related areas of caution in simple language. He applied simple analogies that fit the circumstances of those he was addressing, because he knew their industry and business problems.

Joe Lyman would blush if I told him that he applied the essence of the EPOD Theory and that his legal education was not the primary reason for his success.

WORKING WITH ACCOUNTANTS

Much of what has been discussed about working with a lawyer applies to working with an accountant. The key factor is that the accountant does not make business decisions for you but rather advises you of the status of your business based on the review of your financial documents and situations. The accountant can point out, for example, possible tax liabilities or the need for working capital.

Don't get in the habit of counting on accountants (or any other retained professionals) to do things that they are not qualified to do or can't do. For example your accountant cannot effectively document transactions for you.

Anything you do in business must be documented *by you*. If that requires writing a letter to yourself, then make a memo for the file. Once you create it, always let someone review the document or memo later.

I find that the lack of documentation in business is widespread. People enter into agreements, borrow money, sign notes, and complete transactions without establishing a proper backup paper trail. Without documentation of what you do, your risk multiplies.

"Dave, I can't document everything—I am overwhelmed."

Then don't proceed, or proceed with the realization that you are taking a great risk. It won't serve you later to say, "I did not know that that clause was included," or "I did not know I had to file the update."

HIRING AND DEALING WITH CONSULTANTS

Most established consultants have a list of clients. Many have unsolicited recommendation letters. To make a wise decision, suggest that the consultant provide you with a list of his last six or eight assignments, including the principal with whom he or she dealt with in each of these companies.

Prepare a list of questions when calling the references:

1. How long had you known the consultant prior to retaining him?
2. Was the consultant hired for a specific project?
3. How long has the client-consultant relationship been in existence?
4. Was the project completed as scheduled?
5. If the project has been concluded, would you retain the consultant again?
6. What is your general opinion of the consultant's style? Listen carefully for feedback. You will hear information relating to the way the consultant identified with members of the client's company and possibly with customers.
7. Did you acquire critique sheets from those working with the consultant, and if so, what was the general opinion?

Next, meet and talk with the consultant to assess compatibility with you, your project, and your organization. Clearly define what is expected of each other with an informal agreement. Consider whether your associates will be able to relate to this consultant; will the consultant be able to adapt to the "culture" of your organization?

Then make a go or no-go decision.

Share your information. If the decision is "go," you will be working as a team, therefore the information you share with the consultant, as with attorneys and accountants, will be important. Support the consultant with: job descriptions, organizational charts, annual reports, product brochures, product studies, case-history studies, copies of advertisements, company house organs, trade journals, and personnel biographies.

If you are concerned about the sacrosanct data you are providing, structure a simple privacy and secrecy agreement where you are guaranteed in writing that information provided to the consultant remains sacrosanct.

In every client contact, we use a twelve-page profile containing forty questions. Only when the majority of these are completed do we feel qualified to serve the client's need, and only after all of them are completed can we begin to understand our client's value system. Here is our profile boiled down:

GETTING TO KNOW THE CLIENT

Structure of Business

- Corporation
- Proprietorship
- Division or subsidiary
- Other

Management Technique

- Organizational Chart
- Management Team
- Rules and Policies

Employees

- Number
- Grading of
- Morale of
- Feedback, systems
- Interaction style

Market

- Positioning
- Viability
- Competition
- Demographics

Product or Service Definition

- Product(s) or Service
- Positioning

Advertising Methods

- Budget for
- Successful use
- Problems
- Examples of

Profitability	*Problems (Perceived)*
• Current, past	•
• Industry Standards	•
• Projection	•

EPOD TACTICS

• Integrity in negotiations: "I believe your price is fair because you seem like a fair person to me, so I'll be equally fair with you. Here is my problem:_____(state it)_____. If you can help me solve it, I believe we can do business."

The latter works a lot better than a contrived machination.

• If you are a great negotiator or salesperson, don't take advantage of people: structure arrangements that work for both parties. I do business with many chief executive officers who are lawyers by training but are practicing business executives or entrepreneurs by vocation. They understand contracts and legal terminology, but they also have a knack for business. Fortunately, many of them recognize the value of producing clear, succinct agreements.

• Whenever possible, write it down, even if it is three paragraphs on ruled paper. Date it, initial it, and ask each party to take a copy. When you renegotiate, pull out your original agreements. THE PALEST INK IS BETTER THAN THE MOST REMARKABLE MEMORY.

• If you strike an agreement over the phone, confirm it by letter. Be brief but distinct. Ask the other party to read it, initial it, and return it.

• Don't confuse intellect and the ability to transmit information.

• A lawyer is running a business. So evaluate carefully: Who benefits most from the advice you receive, you or the lawyer?

• Remember that their business is giving legal advice, however they really want to give personal and business advice. Check their business habits or personal lives if you intend to take the nonlegal advice they offer.

• The next time you visit your attorney, accountant, consultant, or medical doctor, dentist, or any other professional service provider, grade him on his interaction skills and determine how you really feel about the service provided.

These professionals serve you in a technical capacity, and the quality of those skills is important. Added to that, assess how much they care about you as a person, and whether you feel good about your interaction with them.

THE EXTRA TOUCH

The next two chapters discuss that elusive, extra something that many effective individuals seem to possess. Chapter 9, "Movers and Shakers," goes behind the scenes to reveal how some people are able to take what others would regard as bad luck or a depressing situation and convert it to their advantage. Movers and shakers, as the chapter discusses, are not born, they are made. They are people who are willing to take a calculated risk, perhaps buck the tide, encounter resistance, and proceed until they ultimately prevail.

Chapter 10, "The Power of EPOD Speeches," reaches into recent history to reveal why some leaders, by the sheer force of their speaking ability—not great intellect or military prowess—were able to command nations. It traces the components of powerful speaking, using the four EPOD elements, providing a host of contemporary examples as well.

9   Movers and Shakers

In time of drastic change, it
is the learners who inherit the
future. The learned usually find
themselves equipped to live in a
world that no longer exists.
—Eric Hofer

The four elements of EPOD were empirically drawn from an observation of people in our society who are movers and shakers—people who exemplify high energy, persuasiveness, optimism, and discipline.

When Lee Iacocca took over at Chrysler, no funds were available for normal operations, not even for advertising. One of the brilliant leadership characteristics that Iacocca exhibited was making drastic changes in the company and then selling people on those changes.

When he sold Chrysler's tank plant in Lima, Ohio, (against the advise of his financial advisors) he was able to generate some immediate cash. Interviewed on television that evening, he used persuasive language about the future of Chrysler by stating that the company had more money in its treasury than at any time in the last several years. This gesture greatly raised the confidence level of Chrysler employees, who were justifiably concerned about receiving their next paycheck, the stability of the company, and receiving their pensions and other retirement benefits.

Iacocca's persuasiveness bolstered the confidence of suppliers, who feared that they might not get paid. He increased the confidence of Chrysler distributors and dealers, the people who sold Chrysler products. With his own energy and persuasiveness Iacocca became a mover and shaker for an organization that seriously doubted its own ability to survive.

What is it about Iacocca's style that transmits high energy and persuasiveness? The man can't speak without moving his hands, and whomever he addresses—whether it's a television audience, an assembly hall, or a boardroom group—he looks straight in the eye. Iacocca speaks in an upbeat, assuring manner, in such a way that the logic (or lack of logic) behind what he says may not be assessed by his listeners. When he presented Chrysler's five-year, 50,000-mile warranty, for example, he made it the backbone of his television advertising pitches. Many people who saw the ads bought the concept. Yet who stopped and questioned that here was the CEO of a virtually bankrupt company offering five-year warranties?

Chrysler couldn't compete with Ford or General Motors by offering a radically different car or by building a new plant. Iacocca would have had no chance head-to-head with traditional advertising campaigns. However, his "buyer protection plan" shook the auto industry. Later, he extended Chrysler's offering by introducing the "car buyer's bill of rights."

Chrysler was still one of the big three in the U.S. automobile industry, but their market share was miniscule compared to General Motors and Ford. For Chrysler, the weak third sister of the industry, to take the lead in offering buyer incentives was tantamount to the tail wagging the dog.

GETTING THINGS DONE

Two classic movers and shakers from recent history were Mahatma Gandhi and Martin Luther King, Jr. Gandhi changed all the rules, confronting the British with his brand of passive resistance and civil disobedience. Gandhi used these and other tools at his disposal—the written word, masses of devoted followers, and world opinion—to manipulate the British in ways that eventually lead to India's independence.

In the early 1960s I lived in the Northeast and regarded myself as a typical white, middle-class American. I didn't understand all the squabble about civil rights, and some of the maneuvers used on both sides of the struggle annoyed me. Nevertheless, I recognized that Dr. Martin Luther King and black people had an important cause.

In one incident, Dr. King was confronted by Bull Connors, who was police chief of Birmingham, Alabama. Though Connors sicced his dogs on them, King and his followers chose to sit down and not resist. When the opposition used billy clubs and tear gas, King did not resist. When the opposition threatened death, King said, "We will love you with our dying breath."

When I saw Martin Luther King on television tell his followers, "Do not resist," "Do not fight back," and "Do not raise your hand," I knew he would prevail. Indeed, he had already won.

King was a mover and shaker because he had the courage to make a difference in the world.

I have had the pleasure of working with Dr. Norman Vincent Peale. Anyone who observes Dr. Peale at work readily notes the tremendous energy he brings to what he does. Now ninety-three years old, he maintains a vigorous daily schedule. Peale has a deep sincerity about his work, and this is at the root of his messages.

One of the great religious leaders in the world today, he leads a life that serves as a shining example to his congregation and followers. He offers his message to other people with an energized, highly persuasive style.

MOVERS AND SHAKERS IN BUSINESS. You don't

have to be a part of history, put your life on the line, or have thousands of followers to be a mover and shaker; you can become one within your own organization or within your business.

CASE #18: NORMAN RALES—YOU GIVE, YOU GET

Movers and shakers come from all kinds of backgrounds. However, Norman Rales's story was fit for Damon Runyon. In 1921, Norman, who was three years old, became a ward of the State of New York and resident of an orphanage at 137th Street and Amsterdam, New York City. His mother had recently died from the birth of his last sister. His grieving immigrant father, with little education and even fewer skills, hoped that Norman would at least have a chance.

As Norman tells it, life in the orphanage was palatable. While you didn't have a mother or father to touch, talk to, and love, at least someone saw to it that you had a bed and that your physical needs were met. For fourteen years this was his home.

On his seventeenth birthday, with a toothbrush and five dollars from the City of New York, he was told it was now his time to go into the world and become self-sufficient. He remembers being told, "The whole U.S. is yours—go find what you want to do." So in 1939, without ever having completed high school, he and his friend "Zaz" hopped a freight train and worked their way to California. His résumé is replete with the titles of waiter, busboy, dishwasher, ditch digger, truck driver, and then carnival roustabout.

It was in this later vocation that his travels took him to Florida, where he met his wife, Ruth, whom he married in 1948. She complemented the drive of this errant soul and encouraged him to become a door-to-door salesman for a home products company in Pittsburgh, Pennsylvania. Although he had no credit background and lived in an apartment with little furniture, except a brand new refrigerator on which he still owed $175, at the age of twenty-eight he went into the Mellon Bank to borrow money for a car.

The loan officer, E. Dudley Townsend, took a risk in giving a loan to this young man with no capital, few assets, and no collateral. Later Dudley Townsend was to become president of a corporation that Norman Rales owned.

Norman Rales at seventy is a mover and shaker nonpareil. He commutes between his offices in Boca Raton, Florida, and Potomac, Maryland, in his own piloted Lear jet. He has owned a bank; part interest in the Texas Rangers baseball team; the well-known resort in French Lick, Indiana; the Golden Strand and Hollywood Beach Hotels in Florida; several other hotels; a public corporation called Master Shield; a company called VIPCO; and dozens of other entities.

If you analyze his success you will see that it is based on a peculiar principle. He calls it "givin' is gettin'." When his first business became successful, Zaz was invited to participate in ownership.

Norman Rales believes in returning to those who have aided him. One of his companies (which was our client) was offered to the employees via an employees stock option plan, ultimately making even the truck drivers wealthy.

In 1979 he sought the eleven men from the orphanage who as boys had played on the championship basketball team and brought them together for a reunion. One year later he started taking them and their families on an annual trip abroad to places such as Rome, Paris, and Switzerland. Several years later he asked them to find the people who had been in the same orphanage (since razed, leaving few existing records) and invited them to a party at the Bahia Mar Yacht Club in Ft. Lauderdale, Florida. The party, which took place on the Sunday between the NFL Championship and the Super Bowl, started with approximately fifty people. Now an annual event, last year it attracted over five hundred.

Normal Rales's concept of "givin' is gettin'" is based on a strong business philosophy of making everyone you meet your partner. His actions seem the antithesis of someone who could be perceived as having been deserted as a child. Norman Rales epitomizes the American dream and a strong work ethic. He's a great dreamer, a lover of humanity, and a man who nurtures those around him.

His orphanage friend and companion, Art Buchwald received the Horatio Alger Award in May 1989 in Washington, DC. It is not coincidental that these men, who started out with much less than the average individual, prospered. When you applaud their accomplishments, remember that somewhere, someone else (possibly you) is saying, "If only I had a better start, more direction, more loving parents, some assets to begin with, or a stronger role model, I could have made it."

CASE #49: PEOPLE MAKE THE DIFFERENCE

Let's examine the accomplishment of Ford Motors, which turned around from disastrous losses in the seventies to worldwide earnings of over 5.3 billion in 1988. You could attribute it to increased market share, their outstanding sales volume of 92.4 billion, the success of the Lincoln Town Car and Continental, or the hottest car of the eighties, the Ford Taurus. However, the many accomplishments at Ford Motors in recent years might be attributed to their mission statement and the attitude of their chairman, Donald Petersen.

Examine their mission statement, page 156, of a few years ago and evaluate the importance they place on people issues.

I believe one of the greatest accomplishments of Don Petersen in his chairmanship of Ford Motors was restructuring the interaction process within Ford, which involved the launching of a vastly improved system for interdepartmental communications. I was pleased to be included as a speaker at the Ford Executive Management Seminars, and I was impressed by Mr. Petersen's presence at and participation in the seminars.

MISSION
Ford Motor Company is a worldwide leader in automotive and automotive-related products and services as well as in newer industries such as aerospace, communications, and financial services. Our mission is to improve continually our products and services to meet our customers' needs, allowing us to prosper as a business and to provide a reasonable return for our stockholders, the owners of our business.

VALUES
How we accomplish our mission is as important as the mission itself. Fundamental to success for the Company are these basic values:

People—Our people are the source of our strength. They provide our corporate intelligence and determine our reputation and vitality. Involvement and teamwork are our core human values.

Products—Our products are the end result of our efforts, and they should be the best in serving customers worldwide. As our products are viewed, so are we viewed.

Profits—Profits are the ultimate measure of how efficiently we provide customers with the best products for their needs. Profits are required to survive and grow.

GUIDING PRINCIPLES
Quality comes first—To achieve customer satisfaction, the quality of our products and services must be our number one priority.

Customers are the focus of everything we do—Our work must be done with our customers in mind, providing better products and services than our competition.

Continuous improvement is essential to our success—We must strive for excellence in everything we do: in our products, in their safety and value—and in our services, our human relations, our competitiveness, and our profitability.

Employee involvement is our way of life—We are a team. We must treat each other with trust and respect.

Dealers and suppliers are our partners—The Company must maintain mutually beneficial relationships with dealers, suppliers, and our other business associates.

Integrity is never compromised—The conduct of our Company worldwide must be pursued in a manner that is socially responsible and commands respect for its integrity and for its positive contributions to society. Our doors are open to men and women alike without discrimination and without regard to ethnic origin or personal beliefs.

THE COMMON DENOMINATORS

How do you become a mover and shaker right where you are? Find a way to excel. Learn more about your job than anyone else, and learn about the jobs of others around you. Compensate for what you do not presently know about the job by exhibiting higher levels of enthusiasm, excitement, and dedication.

Being loyal to the people you work for is also an important initial step in your road to becoming a mover and shaker. When bosses and top managers know that you are loyal, they tend to be more confident in you. Unfortunately, loyalty seems to be becoming a lost art in the work place today.

Begin transmitting high energy to your co-workers, and you will soon be regarded as someone with leadership potential.

Becoming a mover and shaker often requires developing a style. Indeed, many businesses assume the personality of their leader and thereby accomplish what advertising and selling alone cannot do.

To become a mover and shaker, develop your unique style and personality and transfer it to your business (or your position).

When Frank Perdue says, "It takes a tough man to raise a tender chicken," he is perceived as having personal involvement in rearing the chicken you will buy next week, whereas in reality he simply has developed the skill of projecting believability through the medium of television.

If you are a retailer, don't run out and produce television commercials with you as the lead. Most of those people who'd like to make their own commercials lack sufficient credibility.

Tom Carvel, who heads the ice cream company bearing his name, may not seem to have the voice, diction, or stage presence to be a radio or television announcer. Yet he has perfected the art of starring in his own commercials—without appearing visually—lending credibility and reliability to his product.

When J.C. Penney said that the quality of the suits and shirts in his stores were unparalleled, he backed up his statement by always wearing a blue suit and white poplin shirt that came out of stock. In the halcyon days of the J.C. Penney Company, his simple concept of "value given for money spent" and his appeal to the common man through his own life-style made him a mover and shaker.

If you are just starting your career, to make it in a climate in which people say, "You don't have any experience," you say, "Hire me, I am willing to work harder and do more than the average applicant. Check me out." Then work harder and do more.

Movers and shakers are innovators. Keep an eye on ways that you can become an innovator. In your job or your department, is there something that can be done faster, smoother, more efficiently? Even the most well-established and conservative organizations appreciate innovation when it leads to greater profits, reduced costs, or enhanced operations. If you work in an organization that is growing like the Marriott Corporation or MCI, there are opportunities to innovate right where you are.

CASE #13: IDEA OF THE WEEK

Ira Hayes, a former vice president of advertising at National Cash Register and head of their speakers bureau, strongly believes that success emanates from an "idea per week."

At thousands of platform appearances, Hayes has displayed his large three-ring binders, replete with rumpled pages containing his "ideas of the week." He believes that by writing down one new idea each week, many are implemented and accelerate the growth and progress of the idea "accumulator."

"The movers and shakers of tomorrow," says Hayes, "will be those who have the resolve to write down an idea, despite its source, and to keep trying it, despite any resistance they encounter."

Just because large organizations are generally not risk-oriented doesn't mean they don't appreciate innovation from the troops. Don't confuse an organization's desire to main-

tain a dress code or standard of decorum with a lack of
eagerness to have creative, innovative thinkers on staff.

Regardless of the size of your organization, if you show
upper management a better way—a more appealing
package, a less costly distribution system, a more appropriate service mix, or a more comfortable, flexible, or
salable product—they will listen.

In most organizations, it won't be top managers that
inhibit your innovation and creativity but rather the people
around you. If you are a mover and shaker in-the-making,
the people around you may feel threatened. If you start to
put out 20 percent more product per week or stay one hour
longer or volunteer for that tough assignment, some co-
workers will say, "What are you up to?" "Are you apple
polishing?"

Movers and shakers as a rule remain uninhibited by these
kinds of opinions. When you see and feel the resistance of
co-workers, do not become defensive. Movers and shakers
are risk-oriented people who shake off the negativism of
others around them.

How do you know if you are a mover or shaker? You are
one if you are willing to encounter resistance and
proceed.

Suppose you would like to accelerate your career growth,
get more recognitions from the boss, or receive a large
raise. First, write your goals down on paper. Then consider
this key question:

What will you offer in order to get what you want?

Will you start work an hour earlier and leave an hour
later? Take a training course? Read a key text? Spend time
with mentors or junior associates? The extra effort might

involve spending less time at lunch and not taking that afternoon coffee break, or volunteering for an assignment that scares you a little. To become a mover and shaker, you must give 110 percent, offer ideas, suggestions, and problem solutions, and improve your working relationship with those around you.

You don't have to be a workaholic. Rather, pay attention to those things that will help to accelerate the progress you make toward goals. Draw upon your discipline to be more productive during the time that you are at work.

Consider the expressed and unexpressed needs of your boss. He may appreciate someone who makes an extra effort or who can operate without constant supervision.

CASE #50: THE MASTER OF INTERROGATION

Dick Callaway was the director of marketing for the building products division of Kaiser Aluminum when I was retained by them as a consultant. There were significant challenges in constructing a marketing plan in a newly established market with many new products and fierce competition.

I proposed a broad series of training seminars for their sales, technical, and branch management personnel. The program included their involvement at industry and trade shows as well as participation in various trade associations. I also proposed taking one person from their group with me on a fact-finding mission to various dominant Eastern and Midwestern markets.

The company liked the idea and approved the plan. It was Callaway's responsibility to select those on his staff to fill each of the areas of representation within the plan. When it came to the tour of markets, he volunteered himself, and the two of us set off on his educational tour.

In two weeks, we flew or drove to keep over forty appointments to talk to distributors, dealers, and builders. We collected survey data and recorded information with the permission of those with whom we spoke.

Callaway was a top-flight executive with major national responsibility, yet he seldom mentioned his work or his company during our interviews. Instead, he concentrated on asking questions that gave him insights into the world of his prospects and customers.

He would ask a question and maintain complete attention no matter how the respondent wandered or how insignificant the content may have seemed.

He kept a pad and pencil handy and took frequent notes, for which he always asked permission prior to the interview. Frequently, he would answer questions about himself or his company by giving sparse replies, then adding, "However, your business is so interesting, I'd like to know . . . ," and we would be right back to data gathering.

If the respondent spoke of a particular project, business form, or method, he might ask to see it, or he would request copies of advertising and sales aids. He never interrupted and showed great enthusiasm toward each response no matter how minute.

I have seen great trial lawyers extract information from witnesses using the leverage of the courtroom rules, yet not be as effectively as Callaway. At day's end, he dictated his findings and suggestions for follow-up on his portable dictating equipment.

He treated the twenty-three appointments at the end of our first week with all the gusto of the first. At the completion of our tour, we had an abundance of data that was useful to the marketing plan.

The greatest benefit, however, was that Dick Callaway had a complete understanding of the various markets, customers, and problems his sales, advertising, production, and technical staffs would face. Callaway's diligence enabled him to be a mover and shaker within his company and to his staff.

MOVING AND SHAKING IN THE SPEAKING PROFESSION

Some twenty years ago I decided that when making corporate speeches I'd always include music and mood lighting and stand away from the lectern. In my own company, I had no problem doing this because, of course, I was the boss. But as a by-product of my consulting business, I was giving about forty paid speeches annually.

The first time an association sought me for a speech, I told them about my innovative presentation style, and the immediate response was, "We're looking for a speech, not a show." I lost a number of speaking engagements among meeting planners who did not want to take a chance.

Once, I was booked by the regional office of a national typewriter manufacturer. After the date had been reserved, I was asked to visit the regional office and offer a minipresentation of the one scheduled (In those days I would make this presentation trip; today I would not.)

The vice president of the division sat and listened to me. Midway through, he said, "Do I understand that you are going to have music at the beginning and the end, want to raise and lower the lights, and want a spotlight at the end?" I said, "Yes." He thanked me. Subsequently he cancelled my speaking engagement. This embarrassed the meeting planner and disrupted my own schedule because I had already booked the date.

It's funny, people go to a movie and do not think anything about hearing music as the opening credits role, attend a church service and automatically accept that organ music will be used to help lift spirits, or step on an elevator with soft, indistinguishable music in the background and don't think twice about it. Throughout the ages, music has been used to create different moods and different effects. Yet when I mentioned that my presentation included music, many meeting planners reacted as if I were introducing the plague.

I questioned whether or not I was on the right track, because I knew I'd lose other bookings. Back then I hadn't seen anyone else use music or a change of lighting in a speech. This was my innovation; it felt right for me and I believed it would be right for audiences.

Other cancellations came in those early years. It wasn't always possible to determine whether my innovative style was the reason—not everyone was candid. But undoubtedly there were many times in which I didn't even receive a call because I had been rejected in advance.

As word of mouth regarding my presentation began to spread, I was booked more often. Among those who hired me there was often significant resistance right up to the time they could observe audience reaction, which was very favorable. Only then did resistance begin to melt away. Today much of my business consists of giving speeches and producing training videos. My use of music, varied lighting, different props, and theatrics is not only accepted but acclaimed.

In August 1988, I keynoted the annual convention of Toastmasters International in Washington, D.C., which included a gathering of delegates from forty countries and a total audience of over four thousand people. Many attendees made speeches as frequently as I do, and this was an audience that had heard everything and everybody concerning platform techniques.

My address was on the EPOD Theory and drew upon the four dimensions—energy, persuasiveness, optimism, and discipline—to describe what makes some speakers better than others.

Although toastmasters training teaches the use of a lectern and has a prescribed introduction and closing technique, I held true to my style, which includes a presentation from center stage with a hand microphone, special lighting, and music. The fifty-five-minute speech was endorsed as one of the best that those at the convention had ever seen. Over ten thousand cassettes of the recorded presentation sold within ninety days after the convention.

The Toastmasters is an organization of movers and shakers. Toastmasters has over 140,000 members in 6,500 clubs, in 61 countries. Many members are movers and shakers who used speaking as a vehicle to enhance their career or business. To learn more about Toastmasters, contact

> Mr. T. McCann, Executive Director
> Toastmasters International
> P. O. Box 10400
> Santa Ana, CA 92711, USA

No matter what you are trying to accomplish, maintain a firm belief in your ideas, bring the greatest amount of energy to them, and be willing to endure the indignities that may result. Movers and shakers stick with an idea or system longer than anyone else.

RISK AND THE MOVER AND SHAKER

Large organizations do not tend to be risk-oriented. One may look at all the money that corporations pay to acquire a new division and regard this as a risk. But where is the risk? The big corporations often use shareholders' money. If the new division fails, the corporation usually can recoup most of its investment—they will minimize their losses and spin it off.

In 1959, Ford produced and failed with the Edsel, considered one of the classic blunders in U.S. corporate history. Ford closed down the division and suffered a loss of hundreds of millions of dollars, including investments in advertising, machinery, tooling, and parts. After they ceased manufacturing the Edsel, however, Ford still had the same land, equipment, spare parts, and people—all transferable within the corporation. The inventory was quickly sold off. Their dealers were given other products to sell.

Examining the long-term dissolution of the Edsel division in light of the corporation's overall earnings reveals that it was not that much of a risk. Yet the Ford Edsel is still seen as a high-risk, classic failure among corporations.

Risk orientation generally starts in mid-sized companies, is more prevalent in medium- to small-sized companies, and is the bailiwick of entrepreneurs and movers and shakers.

Movers and shakers are kin to entrepreneurs. What is entrepreneurship but developing a plan, adjusting it as needed, and proceeding? You don't give up your plan because sales this quarter didn't meet expectations or because you couldn't anticipate all the variables. You can never anticipate all the variables.

If you have a brand-new widget that isn't selling, then show it to more people, and somewhere, someone will buy it. A slice of the market will buy anything if exposed to it.

When nine out of ten people say, "What an ugly design," there is a person out there who will love it. It may take extra effort to find him or her, but that person is out there.

CASE #33: DOWN WITH INEFFECTIVE BUT POPULAR COMPENSATION SYSTEMS

Years ago I concluded that salespeople who were paid on a commission-only basis could not function properly. I viewed commission-only compensation plans as ineffective and introduced a new compensation plan to my organization, which had 140 salespeople.

My system works on a base salary plus commission, incentives, and contingent compensation. It includes performance level adjustments, goals, and quotas for 13 four-week periods, attracts quality sales candidates, and in the long run saves money. In the early stages, however, it was complicated to install.

After ironing out the kinks, I introduced the system in client organizations and made it work. Initially, the system encountered much skepticism and resistance. People said, "How are you going to administer this?" "No one has ever tried this before." I have since adapted the program for seventy different companies. We differentiated ourselves from the large multinational consulting firms by developing an innovative, effective way to handle what is often a difficult task within a company.

We supported the compensation plan by perfecting an effective sales methodology, consisting of six modules, and producing an in-house training film on how to make a sales presentation using this system. We taught people who had never had this kind of training or hadn't known much about the industry. We became movers and shakers in our industry by using a dramatic sales presentation to carve our niche.

THE TESTING GROUNDS OF INNOVATION

Often, arguments about whether an innovation will work are made at the conference table. Meanwhile the mover and shaker goes out and demonstrates that the innovation does work, knowing that the way to find out if something will work is to test it in the field.

Because an idea doesn't initially appeal doesn't mean it won't work. With a twist and a turn here and there it might be ready. Talk to twenty-five people a week for the next ten weeks to see if you have to modify and refine your idea.

The typical inventor of a new product thinks, "I know this will work. I have tested it in the lab and it has great application." Then he takes it to manufacturers or distributors, who say, "We don't see the value in it." Meeting this kind of resistance, the typical inventor will give up.

If he is a mover and shaker, however, he sticks with his idea. He understands that resistance and extended time horizons are a part of the process. He recognizes that a rocky road awaits him.

WOMEN IN MANAGEMENT—STILL THE UNTAPPED RESOURCE

Movers and shakers among women in management today are those who recognize that it is a risk-oriented world. There may be some nonsense to contend with along the way, but the top is reachable.

I started my career in an era filled with nonsensical rules. For instance, you couldn't be a manager unless you were over the age of thirty. I suppose the prevailing wisdom was that you were not mature enough to be a manager until then. Fortunately, today we know this simply isn't true.

In the 1990s, there is still bias and prejudice against women in management. If a woman wants to be a mover and shaker, she has to understand:

Business is mostly a male-dominated world.

Not acknowledging this reality leads to trouble. The majority of managers and business leaders are men, and the majority of business philosophies have been structured by men. This is not a value judgment about the situation, it is simply what is.

Women require leadership positions before they can restructure the still male-dominated business world.

The woman who wants to succeed does not have to give up anything in which she believes, but she has to understand that to become a mover and shaker generally requires patience. During some presentations with executive women in the audience I write this statement up on the board: A woman without her man is nothing. Many women get upset with the statement. I ask, "Why? It is the truest statement that has ever been made." Now, as their ire climbs to a peak, I add punctuation: A woman, without her, man is nothing.

This exercise helps demonstrate that one has a choice: to find disfavor with what one perceives, or to consider new possibilities within the same apparent conditions. Women are and continue to be a major force in business. As they get to the top, they have the opportunity to redefine major rules in a major way.

Happily we are seeing more and more women in sales organizations. At my seminars for a sales organization, I used to see one or two women in a room of a hundred people. Now, among some groups there are more women than men, and the sales leadership positions are frequently filled by women. I did a program for a company that sold medical equipment, and four of the company's top twelve producers were women, including the top two.

If men are noted for courage, restlessness, and originality, women are seen as nurturing, pleasing, and selfless. It is important not to downgrade the latter, since nurturing and kindness are as important as excellence in business. And the best business people exhibit a mixture of these qualities.

EPOD TACTICS

• Businesses which are efficient yet inhuman may succeed for a while, but ultimately they will fail.

• Every manager is a teacher. The real measurement of his or her ability is the degree to which those managed learn.

• Mentors—they are always present in our lives. Understanding how to use the information that they offer and behavior that they exhibit is frequently difficult.

Know when to let go of each other—Mentors and protéges often extend their relationship until they reach a point of diminishing returns. They outgrow each other, and understanding at the outset that this happens will help. It is dangerous when the mentor/protégé relationship becomes one of dependency.

• Many problems exist in our society today. The people who are going to lead us to positive change will have the courage of their convictions. It takes real guts to attempt new things. A powerful executive with courage takes risks and explores the unknown. Strong managers require the courage to shed old ideas and take risks with new ideas.

• Societies, like successful companies, are driven by ideas. The major movements created by Moses, Jesus, Buddha, and Mohammed were fueled by ideas. Undoubtedly they encountered resistance in the environments in which their ideas were first shared. It was during this trial period, however, that they found their following.

Find a way in your company to encourage the sharing of ideas—suggestion boxes, staff meetings, internal memos—and create an environment where the new ideas are welcomed, discussed, and given a fair trial period.

• The front rows are vacant in meetings conducted with only males present. Females, eager to be in the business world, fill up the front rows.

• Women may represent the best untapped resource for companies who need new salespeople. Whenever managements get beyond their bias, they find out how good women are.

10 The Power of EPOD Speeches

If language is not correct then what is
    said . . .
Is not what is meant;
If what is said is not meant
then what has to be done remains undone;
If this remains undone morals and art will
deteriorate; If morals and art deteriorate,
Justice will go astray; If justice goes astray,
The people will stand about in
helpless confusion.

—Confucius

The Book of Lists indicates that the greatest social
fear is speaking in front of an audience. In my first job I
worked for a company that became a division of Reynolds
Metal. I spoke frequently at training sessions; I knew that
most people were frightened to speak in front of a group.
Because of my background in speech therapy as a child, I
was a leg up on most of my peers.

Those who master the fundamental elements of effective
speech often are promoted or elected to high offices
independent of other qualifications.

WHAT MAKES A SPEECH POWERFUL, MEMORABLE, AND EXCITING?

Preparation plays a major role, as does setting and circumstances. Timing can be a factor, as with President Kennedy's "Ask not what your country can do for you," Churchill's "This will be their finest hour," or Martin Luther King's "I have a dream."

While preparation, setting, circumstance, and timing are factors in the majority of speeches made, few are considered powerful, and even fewer are memorable. I have shared the platform with amateur and professional speakers of varying levels of experience, and I seldom classify speeches I hear as powerful.

Power is the thread of commonality that bridges the speeches of Billy Graham and Norman Vincent Peale, Franklin Roosevelt and Ronald Reagan, Lee Iacocca and Buck Rogers, as well as lesser-known, equally eloquent professional speakers such as Dr. Kenneth McFarland and Bill Gove. (Other than Franklin Roosevelt, I've shared the platform with each of them.)

Powerful and memorable speeches can be framed based on the four elements of EPOD.

High levels of energy in speaking have nothing to do with the age, sex, or athletic prowess of the speaker. Dr. Peale, at ninety-three years of age, demonstrates an energy level that could run a generator. For fifty-two years he was the pastor of the same church. Imagine yourself facing the same audience, in this case a congregation, over that length of time without high energy.

I spoke to Dr. Peale shortly after his ninety-third birthday, and he told me that when he speaks, he feels he has much the same energy level as he had at age forty-five.

Alan Cimberg and Dr. Ruth Westheimer generate as much energy as people twice their size. Franklin Roosevelt was bound to braces, crutches, and wheelchairs most of his adult life; nevertheless, he is noted as one of the century's great orators.

Your energy level will be perceived by audiences based on your enthusiasm, projection, eye contact, voice level, and gestures. Don't confuse raising your voice with high energy. As we've seen, high-level energy is created internally. It comes from the way you feel both about yourself and the audience.

Your energy level is usually determined before you speak. Many speakers who wait for exhilaration from audience reaction, while dealing with anticipation and butterflies, waste energy through hypernervousness. If you've prepared your speech, know your audience, and have checked the environment in which your speech will be given (for example, lighting, sound system, staging), then you can direct your energies internally. Relax and observe your audience. Be part of what's going on. Enjoy the moment and drink in what's happening.

Next, visualize the tremendous cauldron of energy inside you, which drives the human body. Imagine this energy converted into your projection, your gestures, and your dynamic flow of words.

> The audience will measure your energy level by the degree of excitement and enthusiasm you attach to your words. Your gestures and overall body stance at the lectern will reinforce their perception.

If you're working from notes, highlight or underline key words and phrases to ensure that you give them extra "umph" when delivered. Many great speakers use the margins of their prepared notes to indicate where they wish to use a dramatic gesture. Practice and rehearsal with prepared notes allows the energy to flow naturally when the speech is delivered, without looking mechanical or overly theatrical.

The big payoff is that the audience senses your energy and sends theirs back to you via applause. The primary rule of energy applies: High energy begets high energy.

SPEAKING WITH PERSUASION

Since persuasion is based largely on perception and not necessarily on reality, you have to deal with your audience's perceptive capability. Sometimes, the most valuable ideas fall on deaf ears because the level of persuasion is so low that the audience perceives the idea as lacking validity. This seems to be a result of the speaker's lack of conviction and sincerity when presenting the idea.

Oscar Wilde said, "The value of an idea has nothing whatsoever to do with the sincerity of the man/woman [sic] who expresses it."

A key maxim of persuasive speaking is "know your audience": what they do, the issues they're dealing with, and the common ground that brings them together. If you take the time to accumulate data on the audience, you can deliver remarks at the audience's level of perception. You can use analogies, metaphors, or statistics that relate to their industry, background, or level of sophistication.

If an incident has occurred in the last thirty to sixty days or, for that matter, something takes place a few hours before your speech, tailor your remarks accordingly, so that the audience hears what you say as specifically for them.

Cite examples and cases which your audience can identify with, understand, and follow. The Greeks regarded an effective speech as containing three factors: ethos, logos, and pathos. Ethos referred to the potential of the speaker for putting himself in the speech. Logos asked, "Is there a logical progression that people can follow?" As long as they listen, they need to be able to identify with what is going on. Pathos referred to injecting into the speech that part of the speaker's life that was painful.

If the speaker's life history or experience serves as an example, the audience identifies with the issue. Thus, most great speakers have a fair amount of self-disclosure in their presentations.

CASE #14: LIONS AND TIGERS AND BEARS

John Imlay is chairman of the board of Management Science of America, a highly successful custom software producer (a public corporation). When Imlay took over, it was a defunct company. A man of unusual talents, he inherited a situation in which he faced a daily battle to maintain financial solvency. He needed to recruit managers and obtain new customers. Yet he could not guarantee that the company would survive the month.

Imlay's key strategic weapon was, and remains, his speaking ability. He may be one of the best executive speakers I have ever heard. He speaks to the company's department heads and managers, as well as customers and associations, in an inspiring, compelling way, using both dramatic and humorous speech and injecting music into his presentations.

Sometimes he brings live animals on stage to reinforce his point. Once, he told his sales force to "sell like tigers," then brought a large tiger on stage. Another time it was an eagle after he urged his staff to "soar."

Imlay knows a fundamental of persuasive presentations: Whenever you can add another dimension to a presentation, you increase the likelihood that attendees will remember the presentation. When you use a visual, act out a role, or get an audience participating, you increase the probability that the audience will grasp and retain your point.

The high energy and persuasive language Imlay offers, added to his unique presentations, help listeners to remember his message for years afterward. Whether it is to raise capital or to inspire his own troops, Imlay embodies the four elements of EPOD. In a high-technology industry where new products and ideas are created and sometimes abandoned in shorter spans than in most industries, Imlay's speaking skills are an adjunct to and supportive of the company's products and its market plan.

It has to be reassuring to an MSA salesperson, engineer, or technical representative who is interacting with others outside the company to have a leader who is so visible and articulate.

CHRISTIAN 1, LIONS 0

In the days when the Romans were executing the Christians, the Christians would be led into an arena and fed to the lions. In one of these events, Caesar noticed that a lion would not eat one Christian and that the Christian was controlling the lion. He ordered a Pretorian guard to run down to the arena and find out what was going on.

The guard ran down the steps and then came back breathlessly, saying to the emperor, "Caesar, the Christian is leaning over and whispering in the lion's ear, 'After you have eaten me you will be asked to say a few words.'"

THE PROPER USE OF LANGUAGE BECOMES A SYMPHONY FOR THE EAR

In many respects, a persuasive speech is similar to speaking persuasively one-on-one. Select the words and phrases that create feelings of well-being in the audience, reduce the number of first-party references (I, we, me), and increase the number of second-party references (you, your, yours). Seek to eliminate phrases that represent value judgments. Words such as should, ought, and must create a distinct psychological resistance in listeners.

Avoid cursing, obscenities, and scatological language. These forms of expression may have their place; however, platforms, screens, and public gatherings are not the place. If you wish to be persuasive, remember:

Hell is a place, damned is what one can be, four letter words are obscene, and references to waste matter are scatological. To use them inappropriately connotes a lack of intelligence or an extremely limited vocabulary.

The common thread through most political speeches today is value judgments about one's adversary. The use of condemning phrases such as "dumb, stupid, clumsy," or swipes at someone's physical stature, age, background, or past may get an immediate audience response, but in the long run, the negativity reduces the effectiveness of the speech.

Persuasiveness is delivering a message that says, "I want to understand you, to know where you're coming from. I can almost feel your pain; I empathize with you; here is our common bond, and I give you this idea which I hope will be of help."

CASE #159: GET YOURSELF IN THE SPEECH

I was asked on a talk show what single ingredient separates great from ordinary speakers. My spontaneous answer was "It's how much of yourself you have in the speech that others can relate to."

Bill Gove showers his speeches with anecdotal material from his boyhood, his career with 3M, family life, and personal reflections. Og Mandino, an author known world-wide, tells his audiences how the use of alcohol nearly cost him his life.

Jeanne Robertson, at six-four, is the tallest woman who ever competed in the Miss America Pageant. She uses her humor to relate such painful anecdotes as the experience of being taller than most boys at the age of fourteen, and how she sees life from her lofty perch.

Courage is required to include yourself in your speech. Perhaps that's why so many speeches are laced with quotes, excerpts and anecdotes from others. "Borrowed material" is so common among speakers that I get a laugh when I tell audiences, "I'm not saying the guy didn't have original material, but I noticed that all his notes were on tracing paper."

SPEAKING WITH OPTIMISM

In a world filled with negativism, a speaker has the option of following the crowd or selling the positive elements of virtually any set of circumstances. You, as a speaker, have an ideal opportunity to radiate optimism and present the positive side of issues that most people do not think to examine on their own.

"Is the bottle half-full or half-empty?" "Isn't 7 percent unemployment really 93 percent employment?" These examples are triggering devices. While it makes sense to be aware of calamities or dangerous conditions in the world, I believe that most people are interested in solutions. They would like to hear thoughts and ideas that show them how to have a better life and create a better world.

> If you are speaking to an audience that is dealing with rapid change, poor results, or adverse circumstances, cite case histories of those who have gained victory over insurmountable odds.

Optimistic speaking means taking facts and presenting them so that the audience can discern an immediate advantage. In discussing statistics as presented by the press (and prior to presenting the "bright side" of the issue), one speaker tells his audiences: "Statistics are like bikinis; what they reveal is interesting, what they conceal is vital."

Speaking optimistically requires preparation. Avoid those who bring negativity to your surroundings. Avoid reading the front page of the newspaper and listening to the newscast the day of your speech, or in lieu of that, take the statements from these sources and create a position diametrically opposed. Your audience will love it.

Occasionally you may get criticism based on lack of fact-finding research. Just remember, the news sources do the same thing. You are simply reversing the process.

The degree of optimism you present raises the level of hope and the desire to participate in your message by the audience.

DISCIPLINE STARTS BEFORE THE SPEECH

The discipline used by a speaker and contained within a speech is not always apparent to the audience. However, the results of discipline, before and during a speech, are the components that make the speech powerful and memorable. Discipline starts with preparing yourself. Do you know what you're going to say? Have you done your research? Have you put it in a workable format—notes or otherwise—to retrieve when you deliver it? Have you practiced your timing, inflections and nuances?

When a speech begins and ends on time, it's because the speaker has exercised earlier discipline regarding the audience, the other speakers, and the meeting planner.

Effective speakers know this, yet the requirements of public speaking are not common knowledge. I've seen hundreds of speakers run over the scheduled time, stray from their subject matter, and break some of the simplest rules of powerful speaking.

Twenty-five years ago I heard Kenneth McFarland recite the three Bs of successful speaking. He said, "Be enthusiastic, be brief, be seated."

Whether giving a major speech or a presentation to a small group, a speaker's discipline frequently begins with a personal commitment. If your presentation is to be powerful and memorable, you have to be in the physical and mental shape to deliver. Any excess, such as overeating, imbibing, or late night reveling prior to a speech, is not recommended.

As a professional speaker, I get invited to many cocktail parties and celebrations the night before. I have seen a number speakers accept all the invitations, thinking that tomorrow the wages of dissipation will have dissipated. However, you can only deliver at a high level of energy when you feel energetic, and you can only be persuasive and optimistic when you look and act that way. Here discipline means knowing when to say no.

THE POWER OF SPEAKING

One of the greatest speakers in the twentieth century was Adolf Hitler. While I do not agree with anything that he did, objectively assessing his speaking capability I would say he had a powerful technique for spellbinding audiences.

He would look for indications of resistance. When he arrived at that point, he would hit his audience with one idea, then another, in rapid fire. Then he would heighten the emotional tone of the presentation to subdue resistance.

Often he would make his speeches at night using floodlights and torches for dramatic impact. He raised his presentations to a fever pitch with his onlookers screaming for more. He turned his language into an emotional fountain.

The basic tool at Hitler's disposal was his ability to express himself, his use of language. He wasn't physically endowed. He wasn't a great warrior or a celebrated general or someone known for high intellect.

Individuals who have high skill levels but who don't possess the ability to speak face roadblocks throughout their careers. Many dwell in obscurity.

Why? Because they don't work on their language capability and harness the power of speech.

How important an asset is it for a business or a professional person to be able to speak effectively? I am almost thankful for my speech impediment because it put me on the right track. I see major corporate executives today who are ill at ease speaking to their own employees or stockholders. Many experience nervousness and the inability to verbalize.

I entered speech therapy in the Philadelphia school system at the age of six, and for seven years I was tutored in the basics of fundamental speech. My therapists hammered home exercises and practice pieces that I had to work on constantly.

Today my speech defects are virtually undetectable. I'm complimented on my projection, diction, voice resonance, and even theatricality. These are the outcome of discipline in practice. Yet the average person would scoff at the premise of these exercises to improve their speech.

LEADING YOUR AUDIENCE

Audiences typically are moving through a variety of emotional states. If they have not heard you speak before, the first state is apprehension. If you are provocative, they may become agitated or irritated.

When you redefine the provocative issue, their own insights make them comfortable. A great speech delivered by an effective speaker leaves the audience wishing for more, so they may be unhappy when you finish. Think of it as four emotional states: scared, mad, glad, sad. A speaker, like the conductor of a giant orchestra, can lead the audience from one emotional state to another. I recommend the Toastmasters organization to improve one's speaking capability. I believe that their training is the ideal groundwork from which to structure discipline. Once again, their address is listed on page 165.

EPOD Tactics

• The real measurement of your speaking ability is to ask, can they and will they understand what you have said?
• It is difficult for speakers not to compare themselves in public to each other. Yet every time they do, the reference given to the audience says less of them and more of the person they are refering to.
• Before you speak to a group, find out as much about them as you can.
• Get the audience involved—they will understand and remember more of your message.

THE HUMAN
ELEMENT

In business, as in life, people make the difference. The three chapters in this section examine the human element of having a great year every year both within your business and in your personal life.

In Chapter 11, "Love Language and Effective Communication," we'll examine the power of language. We'll introduce affirming language and then explore the detrimental effects of value judging, leading up to a discussion of love language and why it is so important in business and in a career.

Chapter 12, "The Human Difference," focuses on the importance of human resources development within companies, and why this simple but powerful component of effective organizations has been downplayed or overlooked so often in recent years. It also reveals how to retain the right person for the job and avoid the wrong one.

Finally, no discussion on having a great year every year would be complete without consideration of the role that self-esteem plays in an organization—the self esteem of managers and of the staffs they manage. Chapter 13, "Self-Esteem," explains that only by feeling good about yourself can you effectively lead others to be the best they can be. Self-esteem plays a key role in effective management, one that has been overlooked for far too long.

11 Love Language and Effective Communication

> The modern method of instruction has not yet strangled the holy curiosity of inquiry—it is a grave error to believe that the enjoyment of seeing and searching can be promoted by means of coercion and sense of duty.
>
> —Albert Einstein

We live in an era when children hear the words *no* and *don't* (perhaps forty thousand times) as a guide to constructive growth. Is it any wonder that despite the fact that we became the most successful industrial society in the world, we are constantly fed negativism by the news media and our elected officials, and that it has become a management style for many leaders of business and industry?

By the time you were six years old you had developed most of the speech patterns you use today. How you say something, the context in which you say it, your syntax, and your very words are influenced by those surrounding you in your formative years. Yes, you will learn rules of grammar through formal education, but the basic way in which you use language is established before you attend the first grade.

If you were raised in a sophisticated environment, it's likely that you have developed a rather broad vocabulary. If you grew up in a less sophisticated environment, the chances are you have developed a limited vocabulary. With discipline, you can increase your vocabulary.

THE POWER OF LANGUAGE

Language is a powerful tool. Corporations use spokespeople, myself included, to introduce new products, new services, and new philosophies or to overcome problems. Perhaps they have just come off a bad year or quarter, or they have a morale problem. Some simply want to accelerate the positive aspects of their operations, and they recognize the power of language.

How do you improve your ability to communicate to others? By understanding the power of words. Initially I sought to have a large vocabulary for ego gratification. When I was younger, I didn't want anyone to know that I came from a poor family, that I had had trouble speaking in grade school, and that I went to night school to graduate college. I wanted to stand out. I wanted people to say, "There is Dave Yoho. He must be from an Ivy League school. Listen to that vocabulary and that diction."

Development of a good vocabulary is always helpful if it is used to better understand others. An inappropriate reason for increasing your vocabulary is to impress other people.

The power of my language is based on a number of factors: how you, the listener, receive what I am saying; with what feeling I express myself; what feeling my message evokes in you; and how you tend to respond to me.

Affirming language is the most effective and has a positive impact on almost everyone. Surprisingly, affirming language is in contrast to most management language; it includes no value judgments. Affirming language is sometimes mistaken as praise. It is not praise.

Affirming language affirms the individual for what he or she is. It is appreciation language.

The difference between affirming language and praise is subtle. When you praise someone you are value judging what the other person has accomplished. When I affirm you, I acknowledge the effort that you have made without judging it. You will want the affirmation again. Most people are not affirmed nearly enough; some have not been affirmed in years, and others have never been affirmed. You want to be affirmed because it leaves you with a good feeling; it raises your feelings of worthiness.

When we receive affirming language, we do not perceive ourselves as good or bad, right or wrong, but simply worthy.

You may ask why the use of "worthy" and its counterpart, "unworthy," are not a form of value judging? The answer is:

When your self-esteem is high, you feel worthy, and when your self-esteem is low, you feel unworthy, but, in fact, you are *always* worthy, independent of how you feel.

There is no value attached to that. Suppose a worker produces eight units per hour, but the average worker does ten. Is he any less worthy as an individual? Of course not. He might or might not have worked as diligently as he could, but he is no less worthy.

When we tell the worker that we appreciate the effort that he has made, we are separating the effort from the worker. When we tell him, "You did very well," there is no separation of worker and effort.

Telling the worker that he did very well only when he has finished twelve units also leads to a potentially erroneous observation: a worker who finished twelve units made a greater effort than if he had finished eight. This cannot be assumed. He might have been under extreme stress the day he completed eight. (Worthiness and self-esteem are explored further in Chapter 13.)

An ability to reduce your use of value-judging will pay off in your business or your career. Let's see how this is so. Suppose you got drunk last night. Is that good or bad? Neither. You feel rotten this morning. Is that good or bad? Again, neither. If you tend to view getting drunk or feeling rotten the next morning as good or bad, you are value-judging these two developments.

If you feel rotten the next morning, and you have an important meeting to get to, it is appropriate to observe that you have made an unwise decision by getting drunk the night before.

"Okay, Dave, why aren't the use of 'wise' and 'unwise' value judging?"

The use of "unwise" here is an after-the-fact observation. If you felt it important to be on time and alert for your meeting, and you are horribly hung over, it is appropriate and not value judging to observe that you made an unwise decision.

If you stand up and yell in the library when everyone is trying to read, that is neither good nor bad, but it is inappropriate: the library is not the place to yell. If you attend a football game and you yell, that is appropriate.

Value-judging is detrimental in business. Suppose you and I have a buy/sell relationship. Through language, if we value judge each other, we are going to experience an immediate breakdown in the relationship. Suppose you are the customer and are calling my company because you did not receive the service that you wanted.

If my customer service representative value judges your language, he will not be effectively serving you, maintaining your business, and fulfilling the responsibilities of his job.

In business, if you place your value system over mine, then you will judge me and that will be a detriment to our relationship.

Suppose you scream over the phone, and the service rep responds by saying, "Sir, would you please lower your voice; you are shouting in my ear." Your response may be "You bet I am shouting." If you don't respond by shouting, you will hold in your response and let it out subsequently. By repremanding you, the service rep has value-judged you and is going to gain nothing.

By saying, "Sir, I can tell you are very upset," he has acknowledged your behavior.

"Oh, you can tell I am upset, huh?" you say. "How can you tell?"

"I can tell, sir, and I regret anything that we've done that could make you this upset." By using this type of language the service rep will be able to more quickly and more effectively handle your grievance, while increasing the probability of retaining you as a customer.

The language that an effective customer service representative uses is not something that comes naturally. In most cases it has to be taught.

Raised in a society that makes value judgments about virtually every aspect of life, people do not tend to use affirming language even when it would be in their best interest to do so.

The Nordstrom's and the Wal-Marts of the world train their people to use affirming language, because they understand the results that it produces. Language is important in preserving relationships. The feeling you have following an encounter with a store salesperson, profoundly affects your feeling toward the company.

LOVE LANGUAGE AND THE AFFIRMATION PROCESS

The use of love language supports the affirmation process. Did your eyes flutter when you saw the word love? If so, you are value judging the term before you understand how I am using it.

Love has been described as being on three levels. The first level, filial love, is what we extend to our families, but it can be developed within a business, church, or neighborhood environment. The most important aspect of this level of love is accepting others and not condemning or disqualifying them. The second level is eros (romantic) love. The third level is agape—the ability to extend yourself without expecting anything in return. This is the most difficult level of love to achieve. Working to get to that level may be a lifetime challenge.

People tend to be uncomfortable with the term "love language" because they associate it with romantic love. As I use it here,

> Love is the ability to extend yourself to nurture another human being or yourself.

Whenever you extend yourself to nurture others, you are using affirmative or love language, which people like to receive. You can use love language to your benefit in business in many ways.

When your service rep responds to angry callers with "I can tell that you are upset," "I regret that this occurred, and I truly appreciate that you have called it to our attention," or "I regret that our actions, however unintentional, created this discomfort," he or she is using a form of love language, which is also persuasive and affirming.

You can apply love language to employees who underperform, are tardy, or have created a problem. If you intend to maintain the relationship with the employee, separate the behavior from the individual and affirm the individual.

At his lectures, Dr. William Glasser used to say, "The more a person perceives that he/she is loved, the less they will interfere with the lives of others."

CASE #266: EVERYONE WANTS LOVE LANGUAGE

I spoke at a prison, to inmates who were incarcerated for the long haul for heinous crimes. When I asked about their personal relationships—with family, wives, girlfriends—it became apparent that expressions such as "love," "I care about you," and "I like you" were important in those relationships. Then I asked them if they would like to know how to hear more of these kinds of phrases.

The way that you hear more of these love-language phrases is by saying them yourself to others.

I told the prisoners that growing up, I never understood compassion. I never understood that if I wanted people to like me, to love me, I had to send it out first. Because I could not express my feelings, I never got any back. I told them about the difficulties in my life. I said, "I am older than most of you, but we are not much different from each other.

"You look at me and see the nice suit and the watch and say, 'He's not like us; he's had all the advantages.' " Then I told them that I was first stabbed in a street fight when I was fourteen and again when I was seventeen. My nose was broken before I was fifteen and many times since. I was hit in the face with a bottle and had several teeth broken in my teens. I have been stitched up on my face and elsewhere several times.

I was in my forties before I could even hug my own son. I had to learn love language.

CASE #314: LOVE LANGUAGE TAKES GUTS

During a presentation to a Fortune 500 company, I referred several times to love language. I described it and suggested it even meant being tactile—touching another person. Following the speech, when the applause died down, the CEO of the company came to the lectern to offer the closing.

He said, "I'd like to thank Mr. Yoho. I do appreciate the enthusiasm and humor that he brought." Then he looked into the center of the audience and said, "But I will tell you in advance, if any one of you ever comes up to me and says, 'I love you,' I will punch you in the mouth."

That same evening I had dinner with the CEO and his board of directors. At the table he said to me, "Mr. Yoho, what kind of corporations have you run?" I responded. Then he said, "I am curious about your language here today. How did you run your companies?"

I said, "Pretty much the way you run yours today: people were afraid to talk back to me and give me any real input. I set the tone and the rules, and nobody would dare challenge me. But then I never got the truth out of them or any openness either. And I didn't get the production that was possible.

"Then I learned this language and style of speaking, and I threw out the safety valve." He smiled. I am not sure he got my message. He was not about to change. He conveyed the sense that love, sensitivity, and nurturing were anathema to his feelings and that he would feel demeaned by their presence in business. He didn't have the courage to extend himself to another.

ANSWERING QUESTIONS WITH QUESTIONS

Effective love language often involves answering questions with questions (see Chapter 7, the section on co-communication in selling). Most people are not taught to sell. Many think that because they know how to speak, they know how to sell.

Salespeople have to be taught to use effective language, because they are constantly meeting new people but using the same language as always. Not everyone responds to the same phrases.

If someone says to you, "Here is what I am going to be doing," and you respond by saying, "Run that by me one more time," that is effective use of love language. What you are saying is "I am interested, I want to listen." If this is done effectively, no one gets upset about repeating what they have told you.

Can you completely understand others based on their one-time explanation of what they want or will do? It's doubtful. Remember that the most commonly used words in the English language often have multiple meanings. In fact, the five hundred most commonly used words collectively have sixteen thousand different definitions.

Even if you are highly educated and use 3 to 4 percent of the 500,000 words in the English language, you are still only using 15 to 20,000 words, which means there are at least 480,000 words that you don't know or use. This means that you can't assume you fully understand any phrase, whether it appears simple or not.

The use of love language helps to ensure that you understand other people. No matter how clearly or how distinctly another person tells you something, it behooves you to ask additional questions to clarify your understanding.

How do you know if a person is really listening to you when you are talking? He could be nodding his head, smiling, and looking right at you, but that doesn't mean he is really listening. He could be thinking about something totally different while putting up an effective front that suggests that he is listening.

People who mirror what you say aren't necessarily listening. You say the bus is late, and someone says, "Yes, the bus is always late." This is low-level communication; little meaningful exchange of ideas is taking place.

To become a good communicator, listen and then ask questions that increase your understanding of the other person's message.

If I say to you, "The traffic was bad this morning," a question that indicates that you are listening and want to understand me even further would be "What did you notice about the traffic this morning that was worse than other mornings?"

EFFECTIVE LANGUAGE

Effective language is measured very simply. Can the party to whom you are speaking understand what you say? If he or she can, then you can take that party to the next level and the next. Most effective communicators simplify their language. They speak on the level at which they know their audience can respond. Here is an example, via a joke, of the need for correct language: At a time of grave crisis during the Civil War, Abe Lincoln was awakened late one night by an opportunist who reported that the head of customs had just died. "Mr. President, would it be all right if I took his place?" "Well," said Lincoln, "if it's all right with the undertaker, it's all right with me."

CASE #77: POWERFUL COMMUNICATION THROUGH LISTENING

The most powerful form of communication may very well be listening. In addition to teaching, Bill McGrane (an apostle of self-esteem) is one of the finest therapists I know, because of his ability to listen. In an individual counseling or group session, he has the ability to give a person his total undivided attention while the person is speaking. If the person chooses to pause or his or her emotions are overwhelming for fifteen, thirty, or forty-five seconds, McGrane allows the person that latitude and waits. Examine how long forty seconds can be by timing it now!

McGrane says that the greatest thing he can give you is his attentive listening. He became a powerful communicator because he listens. When he does respond, he responds at the value level of the other person rather than his.

CASE #406: A LITTLE COURTESY

A customer didn't like the way a bank manager looked at him presumably because of his dirty construction clothes. So, the customer, who simply wanted a parking slip validated, decided to withdraw his money from the bank, $1 million at a time.

The incident began when the customer went to his bank to cash a one-hundred-dollar check. When he tried to validate the slip to save sixty cents, a bank teller declined, saying he had to make a deposit.

The customer told the teller that he was a substantial

depositor. The teller wouldn't budge. The customer asked to see the manager, who also refused to stamp the ticket.

So the customer called the bank's headquarters, promising to withdraw his $2 million plus unless the manager apologized. No call came.

The next day, the customer withdrew $1 million. "If you have $1000 on deposit or $1 million," he said, "I think your bank should offer you the courtesy of stamping your parking ticket."

CASE #414: SELECTED APPEARANCES AND SELECTED MATERIAL

There are many options regarding the type of language that one uses and how it's used. Ronald Reagan made it a practice to personally deliver good news to the nation. When bad news had to be dispensed, he would rely on someone from the State Department to deliver it at a press conference.

We quickly became conditioned such that anytime Reagan spoke, we knew that the message would be positive and uplifting. Perhaps they called him the great communicator not so much for what he said as for what *he* didn't say.

USING LANGUAGE THAT SERVES YOUR LISTENERS

When people ask me to do the keynote address for their meeting or convention, they often tell me that I have a twenty or twenty-five minute slot to fill. I listen to what they are saying and find out what their program is all about, and then I tell them that twenty to twenty-five minutes is not in their best interest.

They say, "Well, how long do you usually take?" I tell

them, "Anywhere from an hour to an hour and fifteen minutes." I can hear them suck in their breath on the other end of the phone because the average attention span of a listener to a speaker is about seven minutes.

When you speak to a group, you compete with their other senses. They may be looking around or have something else on their minds. How can you extend the attention span of listeners? If, at the end of each seven minute span of time, you change the pace of your speech, and give the listeners humor after a touching story and vice versa, the audience will be responsive. (See Chapter 10.)

If you move about the stage, if you appeal alternatively to the left and then the right side of the brain, and if you use gestures and body language, you can maintain their attention. Suddenly an hour and fifteen minutes is over, and no one can believe it.

It is not so much what I am saying—it is a combination of what I am saying, how I am saying it, and how I am impacting the audience. I carefully select the language that I will be using, the anecdotal material, and even the jokes I will offer.

If you make people feel upbeat or positive with the language that you use and the presentation that you make, they will want to listen to you longer.

EPOD Tactics

• The way we learn to use language as children up to about the age of five is the same way we will use it as managers, until we learn differently.
• If you have a new idea that you want the masses to understand, try explaining it to your child; you will get a pretty good measurement of whether your idea will be understood.
• Actively seek techniques that make you a more effective

communicator with others; see what draws attention and what doesn't.

• Practice using love language: extend yourself to others, then listen to how they respond. Practice being appreciative of what they tell you, even if it is not what you want to hear.

• Even if just between you and a co-worker, work on improving interpersonal communication. Use different vocabulary. Use a nurturing tone.

• Earl Butz had a marvelous plaque on decision making in his office. It read, "Lead, follow, or get the hell out of the way."

12   The Human Difference

They don't erect statues to
people who get things, they
erect them to people who give.
                    —Herb True

Have you ever noticed how, when a new coach takes over a team, and the team starts winning, people are inclined to say it must be the coach? I maintain that is it not the coach but the players—more precisely the players' response to the new situation.

CASE #432: INTERIM COACH WINS ALL

At the start of the 1989 NCAA Basketball Tournament, the Michigan Wolverine coach announced that he had accepted the head job at Arizona for the next season, whereupon he was immediately replaced with an interim coach. The Wolverines went on to win the NCAA title. Steve Fisher, the interim coach, who was then made full-time coach, was credited with doing an excellent job, and rightfully so. But was it the brilliant coaching that made the difference, or was it more important that the situation received wide and continuing media coverage, fans expressed deep concern that the team was handicapped by the sudden coaching change, and perhaps members of the team buckled down and tried that much harder?

Similarly, in football, many franchises have witnessed the arrival of a new coach who appears to lead the team to a winning season following a losing season. Most people say it has to be the coach; I say it is the players—how they respond to the new coach and how they regard the coach and themselves. In the second year, the not-so-new coach often does not equal the previous season.

THE HUMAN DIFFERENCE IN BUSINESS

In business, the same plant and the same employees under new management begin to respond and react differently from before and perhaps have a record quarter. This tells me that people—the staff as well as the management—do indeed make the difference.

I shop at Bloomingdale's as well as Nordstrom's. Nordstrom's employees respond and react to customers in an exceptional manner. Sales staffs, however, within both chains essentially are the same type of people, with similar backgrounds, education, and experience. The difference is in the way that they have been trained to handle their jobs.

And the difference is very dramatic in terms of the amount of sales generated. Both stores are very well lit and carry excellent products, yet as discussed previously, you will consistently find yourself feeling better shopping in Nordstrom's.

Individually you can make a dramatic impact on those around you. Drawing upon the elements of EPOD, even if you are less skilled or experienced than those around you, you can make your corner of the store hum.

CASE #171: WORKING WITH PEOPLE AND OVERCOMING A LANGUAGE IMPEDIMENT

Nick Cangialosi has a smile that makes Jimmy Carter's toothy grin look like a frown. When Cangialosi first greeted me, I was surprised that despite being here thirty years—he immigrated from Palermo, Sicily—he still spoke with a heavy Italian accent.

This new client made a lasting impression as I learned of his history and began to understand his origins. Imagine a man with only a third-grade education having the moxie to run a multimillion-dollar corporation that designed and patented a special kind of extrusion.

Cangialosi developed the knack for successfully hiring and directing the activities of a corp of engineers in both production and research. You have to have prodigious knowledge to comprehend technical processes and then interact with engineers and other technical people. Cangialosi achieved his knowledge through rigorous self-teaching (discipline), despite an initially limited command of English. His skill in deploying human resources developed as he went along.

He is a man who strongly wanted to succeed. His father sold their farm in Italy to raise barely enough money to bring his family to the United States. At the age of fifteen, Cangialosi took a job sweeping the floors of a company that he would buy five years later at a bankruptcy sale. To run this business, he had to take on and work with a partner who could speak English.

Today, in addition to being CEO of a company with hundreds of employees, housed in a one-hundred-thousand square-foot facility that he designed and built, he serves on the technical committee of the American Architectural Manufacturer's Association.

At a time when many people decry their inability to succeed because of what they lack, the Nick Cangialosis of the world prove that the self-made individual can succeed and demonstrate that people do indeed make the difference.

CASE #331: NO ONE TOLD HIM TO DO IT

In a letter to the editor of a local newspaper, a man commended a specific bus driver who worked for the public transit system. The writer commented on how the public transit's buses were overcrowded, dirty, and ran late. He cited this one driver by name, however, saying he had a pleasant word for everyone as they stepped on board.

If the bus driver ran into a traffic jam he reassured his passengers by saying, "Well, we have another little problem here, but don't worry, we are going to make it." The writer went on to say, "I find myself waiting for *his* bus to come along while letting others pass by."

Who makes the service difference? The transit system? The bus? The people on the bus? No, one individual makes the difference, and, of course, the people on the bus respond to this driver and affirm him.

A TALE OF TWO RESTAURANTS

You go to the classiest restaurant in town with the finest menu, food, wine list, and music. You are seated and given a menu. Unbeknownst to you, your waiter and the maître d' are having a disagreement. The waiter is somewhat annoyed while he takes your order. Following a lengthy wait, the waiter returns and says, "We have a problem in the kitchen, but your order will be ready shortly."

Another evening, you go to a different restaurant that is nice but ordinary and is undergoing remodeling, so you are slightly inconvenienced. Both the waiter and the maître d' say that they really appreciate your patronage, and they apologize for the inconvenience.

The waiter tells you that the soup of the day is unavailable because the broiler in the kitchen broke down. But the food comes on time and the waiter remains pleasant. The maitre d' comes over and asks where you are from and how often you come in here. Then he repeats his apology for the inconvenience. As you leave, he says, "I hope you come back soon."

Which restaurant will you go back to? I'll bet on the second one, even though the first restaurant has a classier menu, food, wine list, and music. People will make the difference in your decision.

Business success requires dedicating more of our energies to training people and understanding how the affirmation principle works. The coach has been affirmed by the team. The bus driver has been affirmed by the passengers. You have been affirmed by the waiter and maître d'. If you would like to be affirmed by others, affirm them.

HRD (HUMAN RESOURCE DEVELOPMENT) IS BEHIND CORPORATE SUCCESSES

Why do the human resource development skills of Walt Disney, Lee Iacocca, or Richard DeVoss at Amway get interpreted as something else? Disney's success is attributed primarily to his creative genius, Iacocca's to his marketing know-how, and DeVoss's to his unique sales methodology and motivational techniques.

These visible talents are minor compared to the phenomenal success of each of the men in developing and using human resources (HRD).

In my observation of Japanese management techniques, I have found that 90 percent of the success of their methods is related to HRD. Yet the notion of HRD has been around for years in the United States. Why has it been so difficult to "sell" it to business and industry?

Many companies lack the skill and know-how to implement HRD programs, and thousands of small businesses still are unaware of the value of human resource development within their own companies.

Some aspects of HRD are so simple that they are simply ignored; many businesses prefer to focus on complex management concepts. The more complex the process, the more accomplished management appears to be, whether they are or not.

The growing number of MBAs thwarts many companies' ability to recognize that the key to their success is an uncomplicated HRD process that a high school graduate can understand and put into practice.

Besides all this, most people can be in the presence of great ideas and never recognize them simply because of resistance to change or new ways of approaching situations.

The key to staffing your company with the right people is finding people who are trainable. A successful business manager or entrepreneur recognizes that in today's fast-paced society more than ever, it is necessary to train your staff for the jobs they do.

Regardless of the skill levels that they bring to your company, trainable people can make the difference that adds up to success.

If you are hiring bank tellers, look beyond the ability to run a teller's machine, examine checks, and properly handle cash, to those applicants high in people skills, who can make customers feel good about being in the bank. You will have to train all new tellers to use positive language anyway. If you don't, they are not likely to be effective, and hence you are not likely to be successful.

If you want to hire people to serve as toll collectors in tollbooths, find people with relatively low energy and high patience, who do not get bored easily. You want the type of person who will turn on the radio or read a few pages of a magazine when it gets slow, but who does not need to leave the tollbooth or converse with co-workers. As with any position, there is a definite behavioral style of individuals well-suited to do toll collecting.

EFFECTIVE HIRING: WILL YOU KNOW IT WHEN YOU SEE IT?

How do you avoid hiring the wrong people?

In seminars, I often use a transparency that shows a well-dressed man, with glasses and a handkerchief neatly folded in his pocket, sitting across the table from a job applicant who looks very similar. The caption underneath the photo says, "You know, I like your style."

Andrew Carnegie, founder of U.S. Steel, confessed once that he knew very little about the steel business. His great strength was selecting people who had the ability to do specific jobs. But Carnegie was a rare exception. Today all major corporations have human resource departments who are supposed to fill positions by finding the right person with the appropriate skills and behavior.

In evaluating human resource potential, including your own, it is risky to proceed based on a guess or gut feeling. Many top CEOs tell me that they have uncanny powers when it comes to picking the right people. Yet high turnover at all levels of management plagues many industries, and at lower levels, employee turnover is an insidious problem.

CURB YOUR INTUITION. Most employers still use the intuitive process combined with interviews, résumés, applications, references, and other marginally useful indicators.

"I talked to him for forty-five minutes and he has a good background. I read his résumé. I think he can do well here; he seems to be the kind of person we are looking for."

There is nothing wrong with using intuition; it will serve you well in some instances. When hiring, however, intuition alone will get you into trouble.

While you don't want to place someone with a high ego need or temper problems in customer service, you don't want someone who is constantly subdued either. You seek a proactive rather than reactive person who is objective rather than subjective. Is there a way to find the right person? Read on.

THE HUMAN DIFFERENCE IN GROWING FROM SMALL TO LARGE

For a small company to grow into a large company, it takes people. One of the primary methods of bringing people on board is to first devise a job description that precisely defines the task and skill capabilities that such a person should have to enable him or her to successfully execute the responsibilities of that particular job.

This is obviously not earth-shattering news. However, most job descriptions are based on the employer's perception of the job role. To determine if a job description is working, ask an employee to write a description of his or her job and then see if it matches your description of the same job. Particularly in smaller companies, job descriptions are often not used at all. However, even a simple, one-page series of phrases defining the job role and expectations is better than nothing at all.

In analyzing the type of performance you seek for an existing job, start with the people you already employ. I developed a grading chart that simply rates each staff person in areas in which they are expected to perform. I use a grading system of 1 to 10, with 10 being the highest. As

Individual Grading Chart

Evaluate Categories for Each Individual — On a Grade from 1 (low) to 10 (high)

				Name
				Attitude
				Enthusiasm
				Verbal Skills
				Follows Instructions
				Health/Attendance
				Assertive
				Confident
				Product/Service Knowledge
				Handles Leads
				Paperwork
				Organized
				Money With The Sale
				Closing Skills
				Works With Others

with any grading system, bias can occur. Nevertheless, the goal is to record how you view an employee's performance in each specific aspect of the job function.

If someone is graded low in customer relations, work with that person in that one area to improve his or her specific performance.

As an employee, you can devise your own grading chart, which is particularly useful if your employer doesn't use one. As objectively as possible, grade yourself in all the areas that your job includes.

Self-assessment requires personal discipline. Most people don't want to take the time to assess themselves, and they certainly don't want to give themselves a low score. If asked about your skill in customer relations, chances are you have a decent idea as to whether you are good, fair, or poor. If you are fair or below, over the next twenty-one days focus your attention on improving your ability to handle customers. Put a note on your desk that says, "The customer is the key" or something of a similar nature. Don't try to handle too many areas of improvement at once; one will be more than enough.

The grading chart serves its purpose, but the value of the objectivity of an outside evaluation can't be understated.

THE IMPORTANCE OF DEFINING THE JOB AND ACCOMPANYING BEHAVIORS

Your behavioral style is something that you develop in order to deal with your environment. Behavior is not good or bad, it just is, and your environment is unique to you. If you are the eighth child in your family, your environment will be different from any of your brothers or sisters because your parents will behave differently with you. Your addition to the family alters its structure, and your parents have aged since the last child.

As an employer, if you can simply define the responsibilities of a job and then identify the behavioral profile of the person who could function well in that job role, you would have greater potential to achieve an excellent job-to-person match.

When we work with a client who is attempting to bring on board the right staff, the first thing we do is to determine the ideal profile of each of the people they are seeking.

We ask the client, What exactly do you want this person to be able to do? What kind of temperament should this person have? Who will he or she report to? We ask them to make the list as long and as specific as possible.

We suggest that when making their list, the client observe employees who are already successful in the job function. Often they can identify the degree of creativity needed and the organizational capability, responsiveness, stamina, interpersonal skills, and other abilities of the individual who is right for the job. Then we use an evaluation tool to assess various applicants. The evaluation tells us three basic things: How they perceive themselves (a clue to how they will normally function), how they will operate under undue stress; and how they will mask behavior to meet the needs of the group.

ASCERTAINING BEHAVIORAL STYLE

Many private services provide behavioral indexes that help to ascertain behavioral style: how one interacts with other people, how one tends to function in general, and how one tends to function under stress. I use the Performax © instrument, although there are many other valid instruments.

I rely upon pre-established evaluation tools when hiring

new employees, because we are all creatures of habit with deep-seated prejudices of which we are often not even aware. Frequently, we hire those who mirror our manner of dress, speech, or expression, when their skills attitudes, and experience may not match the type of position we are seeking to fill.

Performax consists of twenty-four sections of forced word choices. The total time alotted to select the word that best describes you and the word that least describes you is only seven minutes.

The instrument evaluates individuals based on four distinct criteria, including dominance, influence, steadiness, and competence/compliance, and uses the forced word choice to help determine preferences and working styles of the individuals being evaluated. I use the evaluations both within my own firm and in working with clients.

I advise chief executive officers and top managers to take the evaluation first, so that they can better understand their preferences and working styles and how those match up with other people.

This enables them to better identify the type of individual who is likely to have the right background and disposition for a specific job, as well as individuals who will tend to work more harmoniously in conjunction with the boss's style.

Whether or not you run your own business or department, or even manage others, I suggest that you treat yourself to some type of job-related evaluation tool. It is in your long-term best interest to understand how you will tend to interact with others in the work place and what types of tasks suit you.

The evaluation tool yields objective information regarding your strengths and weaknesses, likes and dislikes, and often reveals information not otherwise easily surfaced.

In many respects hiring someone is analogous to developing a close, personal relationship. When you hire someone, you have to tolerate their behavior, and they have to tolerate your behavior.

To be an effective manager requires understanding yourself: the kind of person you are and the kind of people you can put up with.

Before you can become an effective manager, you have to know what you are managing. What are your employees likes and dislikes? How are they likely to respond under pressure? The time to find out these things is not six or nine months down the pike, but when a new person first comes on board.

The beauty of evaluation instruments is that they offer the potential to place each person in that environment where he or she is best suited. I encounter people who have gotten their degree, entered a profession, even law or medicine, and later realized that it was not what they wanted to be doing. They are locked into a career at age thirty or thirty-five and may spend years doing what they don't want to be doing.

If we assessed the behavior of high school sophomores, they could gain insight into the types of careers for which they are suited. The profile would show them what kinds of business and management tasks are palatable and unpalatable to them, and how they would tend to relate to other people.

If we, as individuals, knew our real strengths and motivations, then we could easily find a job that would match those characteristics. In the absence of that information, we wander for years.

We could certainly use a better job training program in the United States, one which enabled people to attend school for six months and try various types of professions for the other six months each year. This would give students a far better handle on what they want to do, before they get their degrees.

CASE #23: HELP TALENT TO EXCEL THROUGH PROPER PLACEMENT

Vince Lombardi coached a great football player named Paul Hornung. Hornung was the Heisman Trophy winner at Notre Dame and one of the most talented players to play the game. When he came out of Notre Dame he was a quarterback, but he was capable of playing fullback, halfback, tight end, and several other positions. Lombardi assessed Hornung's capabilities and concluded that he would become a halfback. As a halfback Hornung went on to become a Hall of Famer.

Regardless of your employees' skill levels, when you find the right positions for them you enhance the possibility of their moving from mediocrity to greatness.

Once you determine someone's behavioral style and place that person in a position that matches it, he or she will bloom like a flower.

CASE #66: FORCE-FITTING PEOPLE INTO SLOTS

When John Lindsay was mayor of New York City, he made the utilities adopt a quota system. The mayor's intentions may have been well intented; minorities and women were underrepresented there. But the utilities begin filling positions with individuals who, in many cases, did not have the background or, most importantly, disposition to fit the job.

Some of these people were placed as telephone operators for the utility, a position that requires being able to effectively handle irate callers. Without the experience and behavior necessary to defuse potentially tense situations, these workers were subjected to incredible stress, and many eventually quit what was otherwise the best-paying job they had ever held.

> Placed in jobs that they did not fit, when they "failed," they began to affirm what they had feared all their lives: that they were not "good enough."

Because someone else, such as a boss, a manager, or a mayor, didn't take the time to place them in a set of conditions in which they could be successful, many lost confidence in themselves, which quite possibly affected their future employment and entire career.

CASE #148: PEOPLE DID MAKE THE DIFFERENCE

Albert Madway operates a chain of dry-cleaning stores, each situated on a busy thoroughfare, in a shopping strip, offering one-day service for dry cleaning and shirt laundering. A key ingredient to Madway's operation is each store's manager, who oversees two or three full-time employees and up to seven part-timers.

Each store is connected by computer to Madway's plant, and he receives daily readouts on each store's activity, which provides a simple means of tracking individual customers' orders and maintaining cash control.

Shortly after the computer was installed Madway noticed that the newest and most remote store in the chain was experiencing the most sizable business increases for four months in a row. The store had an interim manager named Edie. The original manager had quit, and Edie, who had been working at the store since it opened, was thrown into the job although she did not come from a business or managerial background.

She was a bright woman who had returned to outside work after her three children had matured. Knowing little about the intricacies of the dry-cleaning business, except for what she had been shown, she concentrated her time and effort in the front of the store with customers.

Edie attempted to greet each one, ask his or her name, and inquire about other interests. She passed out candy to the customer's children, offered suggestions on the clothing brought in, and encouraged the other employees to do likewise. Whenever minor problems occurred, she called the customers, assured them of a swift resolution, and expressed appreciation for their patronage.

Edie's progression to manager was a quirk; no one else was available at the time to fill the position. Later, when she was profiled, all the indicators pointed to her being a "people" rather than a "process" person, a key attribute in a business where personal contact is of paramount importance.

Like Edie, those who function with self-appreciation (self-love) have the appropriate behavior to stimulate the same kind of feelings in customers and prospects. Many prospective employees, however, do not come from an environment of love and are therefore incapable of creating this environment without training.

An observation of Dr. Bernie Siegel helps to further explain why the Edies of the world tend to be the exceptions:

> "The hardest lesson for me to learn was that most of my patients are not the products of such love," says Dr. Siegel. "In fact I would estimate that 80 percent of my patients were unwanted or treated indifferently as children."

Since apparently a limited number of people are inherently capable of using behavior that will stimulate positive interaction, the challenge is to find those who are open to new ideas and language restructuring.

In almost every case where we are brought in to work on "turnarounds" (businesses in grave trouble, possibly failing), we don't start dealing with products, advertising, or sales presentation. We find that by stimulating the properly selected people to effectively follow our new business plan, we achieve earlier and more profitable results.

EPOD TACTICS

• I am appalled by the number of people who don't answer mail or return phone calls. I answer every letter and respond to every phone call I get, no matter how insignificant it appears. Behind every letter and phone call is a person, and I want them to know I appreciate their interest.

• If you want to greatly influence people, stop trying to change them; change the way *you* interact with them.

• Interviewing without effective instruments to evaluate is akin to using a boat without oars or rudder.

• The key questions in evaluating people for a job are: Can they do the job? Will they do the job? and Do they fit?

• The ideal candidate usually . . . isn't.

• Self-starters are usually a figment of your imagination. *Most* people aren't self-starters.

• Evaluate a résumé only *after* you have completed the first phone interview with the candidate.

• Consider the hidden factors that people can bring to the job role. In many cases a simple test will determine the capability and learning capacity of the applicant.

13 Self-Esteem

Self-acceptance is the
foundation on which sound
self-esteem is built.
—Lilburn S. Barksdale

The stronger your ego at any given time, the weaker your self-esteem. Ego stems from the Latin "I am." Ego drives are based on our desires and how we see ourselves in comparison to other people.

A strong ego is an important factor in personal development and has its place in management behavior. However, when the ego is over-extended, it can damage a growing company or interpersonal relationship. The manager with an overpowering ego often does not consider the opinions or feedback data provided by the staff; defensiveness and competitiveness are more important to high-ego individuals. Yet that is the very type of person likely to be hired for or promoted to the position of manager.

CASE #213: THE EXTENSION OF A STRENGTH MAY BECOME A WEAKNESS

Ted Cochran moved up through sales and marketing assignments and was promoted to division manager.

Ted had been permitted by his parents to be independent at an early age. This, coupled with a strong desire to achieve, made him the type of person who got things done, if not with the cooperation of others, then on his own. He was a self-starter, an independent thinker, and a tireless worker who supplied his own energies to compensate for any team weaknesses.

He could make a decision rapidly and act on it. Clearly, Ted's strength was his self-reliant attitude and behavior. He knew he had the personal resources to finish a job even if some of the other team members didn't.

Ted's new division, however, was riddled with problems. It required staff upgrading, a new training program, and revised quality-control standards. Here is where Ted's strength can turn into a weakness. As he routinely traveled from the plant to various branches, he dug in to solve the problems and suddenly found himself harnessed to a seventeen-hour per day work schedule. Then, while under-staffed and working outrageously long hours, he helped design and activate a new training program, although there wasn't a sufficient staff to implement it. Are you feeling tense just reading about Ted?

Ted's self-reliance led him to actions and involvements for which his division was not totally prepared. He did not see himself as a facilitator, and therefore his hands-on management technique required an excessive workload.

His personal involvement in the day-to-day activities of each of his departments did not leave him sufficient time for staff and planning conferences. Staff implementation took longer than usual because he was not there to make the hiring decision, and he hadn't delegated this responsibility.

After three years on the job, Ted has managed a turn-around. However, in doing so he has had abundant turnover problems and has yet to build a staff that can operate without his heavy personal involvement. He is still working a seventeen-hour day and hasn't had a real vacation in two years. Understandably, he is experiencing some personal problems that, in turn, add to his stress.

Ted has extended his strength (self-reliance) to the point where it has in fact become a weakness, diminishing his ability to lead, and effectively shortchanging his company. His overwhelmingly strong ego has become an encumbrance, but Ted would be the last person to accept this reality.

CASE #216: THE PERILS OF A STRONG EGO IN MANAGEMENT

Margaret Lane has become sales manager of a division of a large computer company and the first woman to be in this particular job role. She earned the job because of her excellent sales record and competitiveness. Margaret has strong ego drives. She is proud that she has attained her promotion over many high achievers competing for the position in a male-dominated company.

She has an intense "involvement" style and places importance on being present and participating in almost all regional and district meetings. With a previous excellent sales record and knowledge of productive sales methods, she uses her own past case histories and accomplishments as the basis for many of her presentations and much of her interaction with her staff.

Driven by her own ego, she strokes the egos of her salespeople, showing no favoritism on the basis of sex. Her company has always used incentive and reward systems; under Margaret this area explodes. Volume increases rapidly in the early stages of her management. She is proud of these accomplishments and constantly conveys this to her team in person, in memos, and in activity reports.

Margaret is unaware of the gradual increase of her ego-centered behavior. The sales force becomes "my sales force;" the successes are related as "my volume." Slowly she develops the perception that her team is invincible.

At company sales rallies introducing new products and

promotions, she extends what her team will sell, and she exhorts her salespeople to show top management how capable they are.

The company acquires a new line of products, and Margaret takes the lead in forecasting how much of it her staff will sell. At management staff conferences Margaret is quick to assure top management that her group can meet the forecast. When her staff falls behind on quotas, she prompts them into extra effort.

As it turns out, within two years the company admits that their decision was an error. The new products are not compatible with the standard line and have created many service problems. The company drops the products and writes off its losses.

In the interim, Margaret has lost part of her sales staff because some of the top producers jumped to competitive companies. Part of the customer base has been depleted.

Now the ego deflation process starts: Margaret blames herself for the failure of her group's sales performance. She fulfills her management obligations, never quite recovering from the setback. After a parallel move, which she interprets as a demotion, she resigns and goes to work for a competitor as a regional manager at considerably less income and prestige.

SHOULDA, COULDA, WOULDA: HOW THE EGO DISTORTS PERSPECTIVE

Highly ego-centered managers don't fare well where downsizing or restructuring is undertaken, and tend to blame themselves for the "failure": "If only I had . . ." "I should have known . . ." "I could have . . ." Because of Margaret's positive and upbeat (but ego-driven) outlook, she was unable to acknowledge the reality that she did not fail, the program plan and product sales decision failed.

Highly ego-centered managers often perceive themselves and their tasks as one. Their successes or failures are the measure of how they feel about themselves, and they think of themselves as what they do, not as who they are.

We tend to place a high value on ego development in management. Yet a highly ego-centered approach limits what we can hear and perceive from others, and the ability to discern and value the position of others. A high ego is reflected in one's perception of self-importance and an attitude of invulnerability.

The ego-centered salesperson striving to make a powerful impression and fulfill his or her own needs cannot hear the buying signals or catch hidden meanings in the prospect's language. The high-ego sales manager doesn't consider the opinions or feedback data provided by the sales staff. He or she listens but does not hear.

While the ego is an important factor in personal development, and it has a place in management behavior, it is nonetheless a damaging factor in management development when over-extended. There is a saying from zen that is apropos: The ego is the source of all pain.

If you see someone with a more expensive car than you own, your ego may prompt you to want to compete with the person in another area, where you can win. If someone is telling you about his accomplishments and you find yourself wanting to change the conversation, to inject something about your own accomplishments, your ego is at work.

If you are able to view or hear about the skills of another and acknowledge those skills, without making judgments, then your self-esteem is high and your ego drive is not dominating your perceptions.

To get the most out of a relationship, when another person finishes telling you about his accomplishment, ask him a question about it. When you employ a way to interact with the other person and learn more about what he or she is doing, you are also demonstrating your high self-esteem.

THE BEHAVIORAL TREE

What feeds your level of self-esteem? The answer is the degree to which you perceive that you are loved (not necessarily the degree to which you *are* loved). When your self-esteem is high, you are assuming you are liked, loved, and respected.

At lectures, I draw on the board a behavior tree. Picture if you will a tree growing in a soil called self-esteem. Each of the tree limbs represents one of your skills or an aspect of your behavior. One of the limbs is creativity.

If your self-esteem is high then your creativity is exhibited through your ability to undertake creative problem solving for yourself or others.

You might use your creativity to improve life on the planet, solve an arithmetic equation, help others be more productive, or complete a puzzle.

If your self-esteem is low, your creativity will be manifested in other ways.

It might be exhibited by getting through the workday doing as little as possible or by trying to get ahead by downgrading others. The high-self-esteem child draws a beautiful picture in art class; the low-self-esteem child paints graffiti or an expletive on the side of a subway car. The low-self-esteem child doesn't feel good about him or herself; he or she doesn't feel loved or cared about. This child may not see a way out. He or she uses creativity to break into your car, which this individual has learned to do in under fifty seconds. Although it is difficult for most of us to perceive them as such, graffiti and theft are forms of creativity at work.

As with creativity, the other behaviors on the behavioral tree are fed by your level of self-esteem. The perception of being loved or not being loved becomes reality. The skilled and talented person will act out the hurt and pain that accompanies the perception of not being loved. Once managers understand the problems and conditions of low self-esteem, they tend to take a different approach in managing.

EGO VERSUS SELF-ESTEEM IN MANAGEMENT

Self-esteem plays an important role in management. If you are a sales manager, for example, an important realization is that you are not managing sales, you are managing people. To manage people effectively, you need to find out what makes them function at a high level of productivity.

To be effective as a sales manager, ask questions of your staff, listen to their responses, then ask more questions so that your dialogue becomes an ongoing process.

The high-ego sales manager frequently uses phrases such as "Let me tell you what I see," "I'll tell you what I do," "Let me tell you how I approach this." The sales manager with high self-esteem listens long and carefully to his or her people and asks questions that extend the exchange of information. In this manner, the effective sales manager supports the sales staff and helps them to become more productive.

The sales manager whose ego is in the way constantly imposes his or her way of doing things on salespeople. When a salesperson describes tackling a job by doing ABC, the high-ego sales manager is apt to instruct the salesperson to use method DEF.

There is no love in criticism.

The manager with high self-esteem lets the salesperson talk as much as he or she needs to, although this manager also learns to limit the salesperson's use of the manager's time and personal resources. This manager knows that each person's observations, thoughts, and feelings are nurtured through an outlet for expression. The high self-esteem manager has no need to cut off or restrict the communication of his or her staff.

A high-self esteem manager can enter a department or division and help its people to perform at a higher level even if they have low self-esteem.

CASE #120: TALKING ABOUT FEELINGS

Ed and Ellen Jarvik run a successful chain of furniture and home decorating centers with an in-store sales force of thirty and a field sales force of twenty. When Ed took over the business from his father, the company's founder, there were two stores. Five years after Ed married Ellen, she assumed a major role in the business, and they expanded to four stores and into the home decorating sales force concept.

The Jarviks alternate in directing the activities of the salespeople; both Ed and Ellen fully understand the challenges and obstacles of the sales roles. When it comes to getting the highest level of performance from the salespeople, however, Ellen has been more effective, even though Ed has had more experience and a wider background in sales training and management.

Ellen shows an interest in the feelings of the sales staff;

she openly asks about feelings when policy changes are necessary, schedules are revised, and goals and quotas are structured. Above all, she listens to the responses.

In my opinion (regularly stated to large audiences) women are easier to train as managers because of their relative ease in dealing with management issues related to feelings.

Talking about feelings to establish a more productive environment is still a provocative issue to older, more experienced managers. Many men have a difficult time talking about their true feelings, and they find it difficult to listen to and accept the feelings of others. Often a newer manager who isn't making the transition from previous styles of sales management to the concept of "let's talk about feelings" is more comfortable with it.

THE HAZARDS OF OFFERING PRAISE INSTEAD OF ACKNOWLEDGMENT

When you say, "Fred, I know you can do *better*," you think you are prompting Fred to do *better* and to have or maintain high self-esteem. That statement, however, is a value judgment and tends to diminish Fred's self-esteem because it does not acknowledge him as an individual and his efforts as a task.

Ideally self-esteem is unaffected by, and independent of, someone else's values. If I have high self-esteem, how can what you say affect me? However, through behavioral kinesiology, we know that what someone says often does have positive or negative impact on another person.

A popular management book of several years ago recommended "catching somebody doing something right and offering praise." Yet offering praise conveys the message "I like it when you do the things I want you to do." The implied message is "I dislike it when you do other things."

Conversely, if someone did something considered "wrong," managers were advised to offer a reprimand of the behavior, not the person. As well-intentioned as this advice is, I believe it is misguided because it has a "hook" that says, "I'm happy with you because of what you did (or how you did it)."

In her book *Prisoners of Childhood* (Basic Books, 1981), Dr. Alice Miller discusses analysis with high achievers or people who regard themselves as being high achievers. She says,

> It is one of the turning points in analysis when the narcissistically disturbed patient comes to the emotional insight that all the love he has captured with so much effort and self-denial was not meant for him as he really was, that the admiration for his beauty and achievements was aimed at this beauty and these achievements, and not at the child himself. In analysis, the small and lonely child that is hidden behind his achievements wakes up and asks: "What would have happened if I had appeared before you, bad, ugly, angry, jealous, lazy, dirty, smelly? Where would your love have been then? And I was all these things as well. Does this mean that it was not really me whom you loved, but only what I pretended to be? The well-behaved, reliable, empathic, understanding, and convenient child, who in fact was never a child at all? What became of my childhood? Have I not been cheated out of it? I can never return to it. I can never make up for it. From the beginning I have been a little adult. My abilities—were they simply misused?"

Self-esteem means that an individual has self-acceptance that is based on a value system that does not require accomplishments. In a management environment, if I am a self-loving, self-accepting individual, then I can transmit this to other people.

I can accept you. One of your skills or a particular behavior may require attention, but I accept you as a person, and I avoid value-judging phrases. The people who get the most out of those with whom they interact are working from levels of high self-esteem and self-acceptance.

This is one of the most complex and paradoxical issues I address in management training. Praise and affirmation are separated by a fine line. Affirmation is productive and praise is counterproductive. I recommend reviewing Dr. Miller's above comments for the next month. Many of your views may change on the way job appraisals and evaluations are conducted, or honors and incentives given.

INCREASING SELF-ACCEPTANCE

If high self-esteem is equated with the perception of being loved, how do you increase that feeling? You begin by accepting yourself, which, in essence, means loving yourself. Then you acknowledge that you can change your actions by changing your thinking (and subsequently have a profound effect on the actions of others).

Affirmations support increased self-acceptance:

I am a unique and precious being created by God for very special purposes. I am ever doing the best I can. I am ever growing in love and awareness.

"Let's back up a moment, Dave. You say that I am ever doing the best I can. I don't think that's the case. I wasn't doing the best I could do yesterday." Sure you were; to know better is not to do better. *"I didn't run the best race."* Yes you did, and you may run faster tomorrow. *"I didn't make the wisest decision."* Yes you did. If you had known how to do better, you would have. At that moment, you employed all of your resources and perceptions and concluded "This is what I know; this is what I'm offering."

If you want to be an effective manager or an effective person, when dealing with others, first choose self-acceptance.

Nothing here implies that as a manager or individual you will accept shoddy performance or less than your policy or standards dictate. However, the manner in which you perceive and address others on performance issues impacts the way others feel about themselves. Performance can seldom be improved if someone's feelings are denigrated or his value system is ridiculed. Feelings, especially feelings about the self, have a strong impact on an individual's performance.

YOU CAN CHANGE YOUR PERCEPTION OF RELATIONSHIPS WITH OTHERS

My father is dead and gone, and I can't do much about what actually went on between us. He never said, "I love you" or "I care about you," and he seldom touched me. But I can acknowledge that in his own way, he was doing the best he could. I can understand that he had very low self-esteem. How could he transmit feelings of high self-esteem to me?

I have to accept the relationship I had with my father as the best that either of us could do at that time, under those conditions. I can't ask him to change his words or actions. My perception of our relationship is all that I have to work with, and our father-son relationship is the only one I have. To belabor its inequities or to value-judge my father hampers my ability to increase the intensity of my love for others.

When I feel right about myself and what has transpired in my life, then I am able to have high self-esteem and to transmit high energy to others. When managing, I can help each of my staff members to be more productive.

THE QUIET STRENGTH OF SELF-ACCEPTANCE

The most outgoing, macho, irreverant, and aggressive people on television, in all likelihood, in real life would be products of low self-esteem. Yet they come off as very expressive and entertaining. They have the ability to get people to watch and listen to them. This doesn't mean that they are secure people.

The outgoing television host is analogous to the tough guy you meet in business. You walk into a room and encounter someone sitting at a table figuratively flexing his muscles, dispensing the message "Cross me once and you're dead" or "Negotiate with me and you'll lose." A second person sits at the table very calmly, not lethargic, but relaxed.

Both individuals often find themselves in challenging situations. Ask yourself who is really the stronger negotiator of the two. I would tend to choose the second person. He has confidence in himself and doesn't have to prove himself or make a display to convince others of his power.

He is secure, and chances are his plans are proactive rather than reactive. In the long run, he'll do better for his company and the people with whom he does business.

EGO AND COMPARISON

Noted psychologist Dr. Carl Rogers once told me that the root of all aberrant behavior was probably that basic game "mine is better than yours" or the reverse, "yours is better than mine"—the process of comparison.

Early in life we are taught to be competitive. Later we

tend to over-extend that competitiveness, and it turns into a constant comparison with others. What value is there in comparing yourself—what you have accomplished, earned, owned, or done—with other people? If you draw satisfaction from comparison with others, what does that say about your value system? That you are pleased when you exceed the accomplishments or capabilities of someone else?

> The key to self-acceptance, indeed to happiness, and certainly to having a great year every year, is to practice continual self-acceptance—right now, right here, this moment.

With comparison, the odds are that many times you will feel good about the comparison, that you have superior capabilities to someone else. Many times, however, the comparison is not going to be to your favor. Why settle for fifty-fifty? Avoid comparison, and you can feel good about yourself nearly all the time.

There are people who feel good about themselves most of the time. They don't have down days or participate in negative talk. They also avoid disruptive chemicals such as nicotine, caffeine, white flour, sugar, and fried foods. I am fortunate to be one of those people.

I didn't start out that way. It was only through trial and error, research and observation, that I came to the EPOD Theory and learned how it is possible to feel good about myself. Yes, I sometimes feel rushed and angry and down. But you will seldom see those states linger for more than a few moments.

FROM SELF-ACCEPTANCE TO NOT VALUE-JUDGING OTHERS

After self-acceptance, what else can you do to raise your self-esteem? Stop value-judging—a very difficult thing to do. If you are thin and you see somebody who is fat, if you observe someone with a different religion or philosophy from yours, or someone using language that you don't approve of, will you value-judge that other person? All name calling, deprecating statements, and put-down humor is value-judging. The instant you value-judge, however, your self-esteem is going to decrease.

Abraham Maslow wrote that self-actualization is the epitome of self-expression, being all that one is capable of being. After years of study, he concluded that very few people actually achieve self-actualization. Few people ever exercise their highest level of potential. Eliminating value-judging may seem, or be, an impossible goal to achieve. Yet by attempting it you can activate higher levels of self-esteem. The attempt itself is a fruitful exercise, and any level of the attempt yields a payoff.

Continually reducing value judgment, to whatever degree, is a powerful catalyst in human growth.

EPOD TACTICS

• When you teach, emulate Socrates. He asked more, listened more, taught more, yet said less.
• To receive valid information regarding what works effectively in an environment, eventually you have to deal with feelings. All feelings are valid because they belong to the possessor. You *do not* know how someone feels until they tell you. Saying "I know how you feel" is invalid.
• If you want to understand your employees or your associates, let them talk about their childhood and growing up. What you are looking at now is a larger version of what they were.
• Retain some of your "child." It is helpful when you want to encourage creativity and spontaneity.
• The best way to get others to use new behavior is to adopt

the behavior yourself first. Then you become a model for others.

• Can you forgive without conditions or justification? If you say to someone "I forgive you, but . . . ," the word "but" serves as an eraser, and you are wiping out all that came before it. True forgiveness occurs without "but."

• The word "subordinate" is denigrating and self-defeating. Think for a moment about getting high-level performance from someone labeled and functioning as a "sub" (below par) "ordinate."

• Hands-on technique for managing people:
  1. Show them.
  2. Tell them what you've shown them.
  3. Show them again.
  4. Let them tell you what they've observed.
  5. Watch them do it.
  6. Tell them what you've observed.
  7. Watch them do it again.
  8. Develop a critique together.
  9. Repeat the process or any part of it when necessary.
  10. Whenever they are having a problem, encourage them to discuss *feelings*.

Conclusion
Dream Your Dream

Faith is believing in
things when common sense
tells you not to.
                    —Dave Yoho

When I was young I had to read *Don Quixote* for
school. I didn't understand it. As an adult, I saw the musical
version of *Don Quixote*, *The Man of La Mancha*, and I
heard the enchanting words of the song "The Impossible
Dream." The words relate to the quest of fulfilling an
impossible dream, fighting unbeatable foes, bearing un-
bearable sorrow, and venturing where even the bravest
among us dare not go.

The words were so beautiful, could they be about a
half-crazed nobleman? They are not. The words to "The
Impossible Dream" were written about Miguel Cervantes,
the author of *Don Quixote,* who at 17 was taken prisoner in
the Spanish-Moorish Wars. Eventually he was ransomed
with fees paid by his family. Upon his return home,
Cervantes was given the role of tax collector.

When he attempted to collect from the rich instead of the
poor he was again imprisoned, this time in his own country,
and tortured—during his incarceration two fingers were
broken on his right hand.

What are the options of such a man? He did not become
a social deviant; he did not dishonor his family. He wrote

Don Quixote, as a social protest, and it has lasted for hundreds of years.

What will be your social protest? Will you live in the pain of whatever it is you are experiencing, or will you take the opportunity to write your own song, your own social protest? Will you dream your dream?

The EPOD Theory is not a panacea. It is, however, a tool that will help in the implementation and facilitation of your dream.

Of course, EPOD is not a word, and, paradoxically, if you reverse the letters, it spells DOPE. This interesting observation is my conclusion. You have the choice.

And when your day is not what you want it to be, when your life is not what you want it to be, remember, God made you so different, so beautifully different, that even your fingerprints are unique.

You are unique and special, and
you have the potential to
be whatever it is
you want to be

To get in contact with Dave Yoho, write or call:

Dave Yoho Associates
10803 West Main Street
Fairfax, VA 22030

703-591-2490

Bibliography

Beecroft, John, Editor. *Kipling. A Selection of His Short Stories and Poems*. New York: Doubleday, 1962.

Diamond, Dr. John. *BK* Behavioral Kinesiology: The New Science of Positive Health Through Muscle Testing*. New York: Harper & Row, 1979.

Dyer, Dr. Wayne. *Your Erroneous Zones*. New York: Funk and Wagnalls, 1976.

Jampolski, Dr. Gerald. *Love is Letting Go of Fear*. New York: Bantam, 1982.

Miller, Dr. Alice. *Prisoners of Childhood*. New York: Basic Books, 1981.

Siegel, Dr. Bernie. *Love, Medicine and Miracles*. New York: Harper & Row, 1986

Wallace, Irving, Amy Wallace, and Dave Wallechinsky. *The Book of Lists*. New York: Bantam, 1977.

Yoho, Dave. *The Art of Communication*. Fairfax, Virginia: Dave Yoho Associates, 1973.

Yoho, Dave. *Closing the Sale*. Fairfax, Virginia: Dave Yoho Associates, 1983.

Yoho, Dave. *Customer Satisfaction Selling*. Fairfax, Virginia: Dave Yoho Associates, 1989.

INDEX